PATRIOTIC
ILLUSIONS

PATRIOTIC
ILLUSIONS

COLONEL (RET.)
MARK TALBOT

*For Rachel who sacrificed everything
to support my hopes and dreams.*

Table of Contents

Introduction

THE BEDROCK OF AMERICAN culture shifts and buckles under our feet. The Coronavirus crisis coupled with widespread and growing awareness of systemic racism and police brutality have brought this country to its knees. We did not get into this mess overnight and we will not quickly or easily extract ourselves from the quagmire. The original sin of slavery, continued exploitation of vulnerable people, and a crisis of trust in America's leaders haunt our every move. Nevertheless, hope remains. We live in an incredibly prosperous democracy forged in fire and blood. We the people hold the ultimate power when we chose to awaken and begin to hold those in positions of authority accountable for their actions. Educating ourselves regarding the motivations of our current leadership as well as the broken incentive structures which exist across the entire spectrum of our society is the crucial first step.

The most crushing form of tyranny involves controlling what people think, not what they do. It is the intellectual equivalent of kneeling on someone's neck. For too long we have subscribed to the lies promulgated by those who benefit from maintaining the status quo. Heart-warming testimonials about the greatness of our country, fourth of July parades, and a public education system which conditions us to conform have lulled us into complacency. Just sit back, relax, and enjoy the ride. Nothing wrong here. Many of the most successful Americans, for instance, simply obey higher authority without further inquiry. From the time we learn to walk, we are pressured into unconditional love of country. Patriotism is a national pastime. To speak out against America's warts is to commit treason!

I must admit I have always loved my country and am grateful I was born an American. I loyally served in the military for nearly thirty years and continue to support it today. Nevertheless, I see America for what it is, not what I would like it to be. I would willingly lay down my life for my brothers and sisters in arms and my immediate family, but not for some vague and ethereal concept of country. Many military people act and feel the same—an important distinction lost on Americans who feel our service represents a personal favor just for them. It is not. No one but a psychopath signs up to fight and voluntarily die for anything. Those in uniform must sometimes put their lives on the line for each other, but not for you. Every sane military person both wants and expects to come home safely to enjoy the blessings of liberty.

This disconnect in understanding, among many others, motivated me to capture and share my observations in this book which I have filled with unique perspectives. Unfortunately, people do not usually spend much time contemplating foundational issues and avoid taking a firm stand on potentially contentious matters. The days of blissful ignorance, however, have waned. It is time for action. History proves that change requires people with the courage to disobey. Reformers buck trends and challenge the system. We must therefore free our minds, reject conventional wisdom and find new and better ways of doing business. The following twelve chapters expose, analyze, and offer viable alternatives to the Patriotic Illusions which those in power would love for you to continue to believe. Do not do them the favor of lying lifeless on the altar of their corruption and decadence!

CHAPTER 1

Heroes Lead our Military

In most cases, those who want power probably
shouldn't have it, those who enjoy it probably do so for
the wrong reasons, and those who want most to hold
on to it don't understand that it's only temporary.
—John C. Maxwell

I SAT IN MY SPARSELY decorated cubicle outside the General's office dreaming of happier times when the phone rang interrupting my train of thought.

I picked up the receiver, "this is the office of General Mayhem, Lieutenant Colonel...."

"Stop talking immediately!" a shrill voice interrupted my standard greeting. "This is Colonel Klink, I'm the military assistant to the Secretary of Something really important. I need an update on Excalibur ammunition in Afghanistan within two hours. The Secretary has to brief Congress tomorrow morning."

What a jerk I thought. He could not wait the extra two seconds for me to finish my greeting. Something inside me snapped. I guess I had not yet fully acclimated to the continual state of manufactured emergencies and high stress levels at the Pentagon. I had received more than enough verbal abuse for one day, so I simply hung up the phone. If I could not talk, no point in carrying on with the phone call I rationalized. I instantly regretted this decision. My body suddenly burst into a light sweat. I knew I had just screwed up and thrown down the gauntlet with the wrong guy. This was not the Field Army where officers worked out their differences eyeball to eyeball and checked negative behaviors such as unnecessary rudeness. Like Dorothy in the Wizard of Oz, I realized I was not in Kansas anymore. The phone rang again within seconds and it could only be Colonel Klink. I picked up the receiver and waited. Silence on both ends for a few brief seconds. Colonel Klink blinked first.

"This is Colonel Klink, and I'm the military assistant to the Secretary of Something really important (he had to remind me once again he served Pentagon royalty). With whom am I speaking?"

I swallowed hard. In basketball terminology, sometimes you just have to go strong to the hoop. "Oh, is it okay for me to speak now?" I answered in a snarky tone.

"Don't move from your location. I'll be there in five minutes" Colonel Klink barked.

Based on the relative locations of our office suites within the immense labyrinth of the Pentagon, I knew I could turn tail and be well on my way to the parking lot before Colonel Klink pinned me down. No point in running though. Only T1000 Terminators serve the Secretary and my name may as well be Sarah Connor now. That bastard absolutely would not stop until he hunted me down.

Colonel Klink arrived in short order and proceeded to chew my ass in spectacular fashion. Interesting that he could not spare the two extra seconds to listen to my greeting, but he had 30 minutes to find and chastise me. A small crowd gathered to listen to the threats and profanities. Klink could have pulled me into a private office to deliver the beat-down, but he clearly wanted to make an example through public execution. I did my best to take the abuse without showing emotion. As a moderately experienced boxer, I learned a punch hurts most when you flinch in anticipation, so I tried not to tense up. Good life advice across many domains by the way! When you find yourself in the jaws of the beast, just go limp. As Klink flamed on, he worked himself into a proper froth, spit flying everywhere. The old "say it don't spray it" meme crept into my mind and it must have made me smile. I could not help but think about the anonymous bag of dog crap I intended to leave on Klink's desk after hours in his office on prime real estate within the E ring. A nice surprise to go with his morning coffee. For the uninitiated, the Pentagon has five interior corridors lettered A through E running parallel to its five exterior sides like layers of an onion. The Department of Defense's most senior officials have luxurious window offices on the outermost layer or E-ring. An enslaved and rebellious staff officer such as me might enjoy rollerblading through the nearly 18 miles of corridors after hours to pass the time.

My irreverent attitude only poked the bear so Klink made a point of having a private conversation with the General for whom I worked. You can probably imagine he did not do me any favors. Klink knew the mere implication of incompetence or unprofessionalism could unravel my career progression. The previous 24 years of distinguished service counted for nothing. Success as an Army officer dictates that every moment matters. No matter, serving at the Pentagon helped me see the strings at the puppet show so to speak. I resolved to continue in the Army but pursue only jobs which interested me instead of allowing Generals and senior mentors dictate the terms of my service. I had three subsequent assignments and pinned on Colonel, but nothing more. Stick a fork in me—I was done. Working at the corporate level of the Army no longer interested me given the excessively toxic environment.

The experience made me long for the simpler days of leading, training, and teaching young people the art of soldiering—my true passion. Service at the Pentagon on the other hand reeked of political maneuvering, half-truths, absurdly long hours, and ass kissing. Even though I had worn a uniform for over two decades before landing at the puzzle palace, I had no clue why it even existed. Combat units like the 82nd Airborne, 10th Mountain, and 1st Calvary Divisions train our soldiers to fight and win our wars. In my humble opinion, these will always be the Army's center of gravity. Why then do over 30,000 people flock to the 5-sided jackass coliseum every workday? A great question every American should ask themselves. To be honest, I still am not completely sure. The simple infantryman in me believes it might be one of the worlds' largest and most useless institutions, but you can think of it as the interface between the political institutions of the National Capitol Region and our Warfighters. The Pentagon workforce spends much of its time preparing and defending budget requests for submission to Congress and the President. It serves as the Department of Defense's corporate and financial headquarters turning taxpayer resources and political whims into weapons of war and actionable guidance for our Divisions, Fleets, and Squadrons.

The assignment taught me the Pentagon is like a flame for the ugliest military moths. It attracts and nourishes the wrong types of people: uniformed politicians. I very much wished I had never taken this "fast-track" assignment. During the previous 13-month deployment in Iraq, I had made a name for myself and left a positive impression on an Army senior leader. This General took an active interest in helping me advance and ensured I landed a career-enhancing job at the Pentagon as a reward for my performance in the combat zone. Further adding to my professional optimism, the Army had just selected me early ("below the zone") for promotion to

Lieutenant Colonel (top 5% among my peer officers). It felt like everything was coming together for me; the future was so bright, I had to wear shades! As my first Platoon Sergeant on border patrol in West Germany said when I was a private, I sparkled like a diamond in a goat's ass.

Upon redeploying from Iraq, I assumed the job as the Executive Officer for another General in a similar career field. What an unexpected shit-sandwich! Could I get some mayonnaise please to help choke down this turd? The position required me to work an average fifteen-hour day. Factoring in the commute time associated with living in the Washington, DC area, I left my home at 4:30 am and typically did not return until 8:30 pm. The Pentagon was full of "Iron Majors and Colonels" like me, indentured servants for the stars. Every one-star wants to be a two-star, every two star wants a third, and every three-banger wants a fourth. Staff officers at the Pentagon exist to work without boundaries to help their bosses continue to climb. All-nighters, a few hours of sleep on the office couch, two pots of coffee a day, and the constant stress imposed by tyrannical bosses are par for the course. If you do a really great job, however, your General or Admiral might help elevate you to the stars as well. When it comes to Flag officers, it takes one to make one (we call Generals and Admirals Flag Officers because they traditionally displayed a flag with their number of stars on their official military vehicles). The Army's sitting senior Generals unilaterally decide who to elevate to Flag Rank without considering any substantive data. It is an unabashed popularity contest. They also decide the fate of any within their posy who violate laws, regulations, and policies. As you might guess, they protect each other to the greatest extent possible. Generals and Admirals guilty of violations that would see a junior officer or enlisted soldier court martialed and sent to jail result in mere administrative fines or forced retirement with full benefits for the stars. A "different spanks for different ranks" paradigm thrives within the military.

I realized for the first time, climbing to the top of the military pyramid requires forfeiture of all other life interests and activities while setting aside professional ethics in favor of politics. Even being a good parent and spouse would have to take a backseat to service at the corporate level. My wife and children joked they saw me more when I was in Iraq because at least we had the chance to videoconference routinely. Even though assigned stateside, I was a stranger in my own home— the unadvertised price of military success. A few hours on Sunday afternoons provided my only opportunity to interact with my three young children. Reflecting on my decades of service, I never once had breakfast with any of my children on a school day. Most nights, I missed dinner as well. All of my numerous and diverse military positions required me to leave the house long before they awoke and return late in the evening. Neither did I ever participate nor witness after school activities and sporting events. Even when not deployed, the yoke of Army leadership weighed too heavily for me to make time for my children. I look back on the choices I made as a father and husband with shame and regret. I was too caught up in service and my career to see what I had become. What is the point of a job or career if you have so little time with those who should matter most? As many military leaders jokingly proclaim, however, if the Army wanted you to have a family, it would have issued you one. Silly of me to believe it was possible to achieve balance between my personal life and professional military career. Since retiring, I now have breakfast with my 11-year-old son every morning, coach his basketball team, and have time to help him with his homework most every night. All while holding a regular job which pays considerably more than my Army salary. This contrasts sharply with my active duty experience and shines a very bright light on my dereliction of parental duties when in uniform.

I had initially idolized the General and mentor who took an interest in helping me advance. Serving close to Flag Officers at the Pentagon, however, provided a much different perspective. Many worked from 6 am until 11 pm and routinely demanded unreasonable support from their bloated staffs. We often called people back to work with no notice to provide classified information updates for Generals which we could not discuss over the telephone. The information, however, was usually just that—information. On one such occasion, I called three Army officers back to the Pentagon at 9 pm on a Friday night to provide status on ammunition inventories across the force. These updates answered queries from the Army Chief of Staff but generated no subsequent action. A reasonable person, therefore, might ask, why the hurry? What is the difference between having this information Friday night versus the following Monday morning during regular duty hours? The answer lies in the impression the Chief of Staff, the top Army four-star who had the ultimate say in all other General's careers, had of the subordinate General's responsiveness, dedication, and ability to immediately satisfy a mere curiosity.

Further reinforcing my growing disdain for Flag Officers, I watched their behavior leading up to crucial high-level meetings. They demanded extensive pre-briefs from subordinates to cover all possible contingencies which might arise. These pre-briefs compensated for a lack of technical depth and their limited ability to think on their feet. If you cannot make a good decision without being extensively coached by subordinates, you are either incompetent and the wrong person for the job, or the decision needs to be made at a lower level. Most Flags also attempted to determine the equities and positions of all other stakeholders and drove their staffs to gather "intel" on what others might be working to achieve. The combination of senior leader requirements for pre-briefs, horse-holding, and intelligence gathering drive the staffs of our Generals and Admirals to grow beyond all reason. The 30,000 plus Pentagon workforce continues to expand and spill over into dozens of adjacent buildings in the Washington DC metropolitan area with no end in sight. This growth is driven mostly by our senior military leaders' insatiable appetite for information, power, and unchecked ambition.

13

The American public rightfully expects its senior military leaders to be sharp as tacks, decisive, moral, and apolitical. The ones I observed, however, possessed average intelligence, avoided being pinned down with a potentially contentious opinion or decision, and used subordinates to make them look good within the Pentagon's grand Game of Thrones. In other words, exactly the opposite of what we expect and need to ensure our safety and security.

The personal characteristics and motivations of the Department of Defense's senior leadership also drive the never-ending workday interrupted only by the biological needs to eat and sleep. I befriended a fellow executive officer, also a Lieutenant Colonel. We enjoyed each other's company in the rare spare moments in between ass kicking's. This officer kept pace with his General and wanted very badly to one day be a General himself as did all of us slaving away in the bowels of the Pentagon. A few years later, he quite tragically and unexpectedly died of cancer in his 40s. Many military officers, to include me, often ignore our personal health as this is perceived as a sign of weakness and also takes time away from our professional responsibilities. Every General wants an Executive Officer who provides uninterrupted 24 x 7 support. No doubt, this officer ignored the warning signs and the cancer progressed too far before detection and treatment. I wonder if lying on his death bed, did he regret all the missed time with his wife, children, wider family, and friends or was he simply sad he would not live to be a General? Is professional success worth forfeiting everything else? How many other lives have such demanding Generals used, and abused on their way to the top? Nobody in uniform really cares—the big green machine churns on. As soon as an officer or soldier dies, the establishment simply generates a replacement. It is designed to be completely impartial despite outside perceptions. The bereaved families may choose a sanctioned military funeral replete with emotional eulogies and memorial tokens from a grateful nation. The military thus creates a wonderful patriotic illusion. One should never love a person or institution which does not return the sentiment. Fast-forward a year and hardly anyone in the ranks remembers the fallen or their families given the constantly moving conveyor belt of mission requirements.

Not surprisingly, the leadership style and demands of the Pentagon's senior uniformed leaders shape the behaviors and attitudes of the supporting workforce. Every experienced Commander knows his unit will eventually adopt his personality. If you have been in the leadership saddle for a long time and you do not like your team, take a look in the mirror. Toxic leaders create toxic followers who wreak great havoc within the ranks and demoralize even the best subordinates. When a noble-minded and competent leader replaces a toxic one, he must deal with the stay-behind cadre who supported and thrived under the previous regime. Unfortunately, even well-intentioned leaders often simply avoid addressing dysfunctional behaviors because it requires mountains of time and energy. The movers and shakers of the world know they will receive a far higher return on investment by making themselves look good while currying favor with their bosses. Military professionals worship the PIE model for success, short for Performance, Impression and Exposure. Tending to these three variables helps ensure success. Job performance should matter, but no more so than the impression your bosses have of you as well as your exposure to high level mentors who can nurture your career and pull you along. Unlike many other career fields, however, the military implements completely subjective evaluation practices. Your boss's boss who sits at least one level removed from your daily activities gives you a grade based upon his or her opinion of your performance without any requirement to consider substantiating evidence or data. The PIE framework in this case effectively collapses onto a two-legged wobbly stool depending wholly upon impression and exposure. The military professionals who rise to the top spend most of their time tending to these two priorities. Holding toxic subordinates accountable for their actions, therefore, is wasted energy and effort which inevitably makes enemies. When you threaten a person's career and livelihood, their retaliatory measures know no bounds. Wrestling with pigs gets you dirty! Even someone low on the organizational totem pole often has high-level connections whom they will leverage to turn against one whom would hold them accountable. Far safer for the emerging leader, therefore, to simply go along to get along. After all, the next promotion will move them up and out leaving the problem subordinates in the rearview mirror for someone else to confront.

I have seen many secretaries, for instance, perpetually behave badly and ignore guidance from middle and upper management. They get away with poor performance and negative attitudes because the big boss "has their back." This is exactly the situation I walked into at the Pentagon. One General I knew fired his Executive Officer because his secretary simply did not like the Colonel. The secretary and previous Executive Officer had a personality conflict, but make no mistake, the Colonel trumped her in rank by a long shot (for perspective, a Colonel in the Field Army typically commands approximately 3000 soldiers). If the two individuals could not work together, the General should have removed or counseled the secretary. The General and secretary, however, had a longstanding personal relationship so the Colonel got the trap door leaving a lasting negative impact on his career. I held one rank lower at the time then the officer I replaced; I served as a Lieutenant Colonel. Imagine the trepidation I felt upon taking such a position. Everyone who has served in the Pentagon knows and fears the informal power of the secretarial aka executive assistant mafia. These career assistants climb along with their bosses and fiercely protect them while wielding influence with their peers in other offices. Mere rumor and inuendo can ruin a staff officer's career. If one of these individuals decides they do not like you, your emails, staff action packets, and meeting requests will simply get deleted before they ever reach the intended recipients. The secretary with whom I had to work knew she had me by the proverbial crown jewels. I had to play along with her jack-assery or accept the end of my Army career progression.

Toxic subordinates can only thrive, however, in the shadow of weak leadership. Unfortunately, those leaders who make the effort to weed the garden so to speak, inevitably make enemies and do not shine as brightly as the spot-light rangers who constantly tend to their professional images and seek exposure to high level mentors with whom they curry favor. This tragedy plays out every day all across America, not just within the military. The root cause lies in the conscious choices people of all walks of life make to prioritize career progression over doing the right thing. The secretary had the most important quality the General sought—fierce loyalty. She helped him climb to the top and nothing else mattered to either of them.

The paint thus started to flake off the big green Army turd for me. Klink would no doubt one day be a four-star General. Somebody very powerful had hand-picked him to serve in such an exalted position thus guaranteeing his rise to the heavens. He had A+s in both exposure and impression making his performance largely irrelevant. His personality fit the Pentagon mold perfectly and he had long since forfeited everything else in life to "succeed". No doubt his wife and children had already learned to live without him. We should all question the true motivations of people who willingly forfeit everything in life for either career or country. As demonstrated in figure 1 on page 20, everyone has a hierarchy of loyalties. While we may not all agree on the exact order in figure 1, we must acknowledge some people are quite naturally more important to us than others. Many for instance, might place a creator or family before themselves, and this is quite understandable and honorable. The extremely patriotic among us might even put nation above friends and family. The very notion of patriotism, however, requires a deliberate choice of "my people before your people" along national boundaries so it is perhaps not so noble a concept after all. The military careerist who forfeits decades of his or her time and freedom to their country and profession actually has no loyalty to anything or anyone else. Words and protestations to the contrary mean nothing. You vote with your feet—if you are not there, you must not care. The orbits of loyalty in figure 1 then collapse onto a single bubble around self and career. The perpetual state of warfare Americans have come to accept without question requires senior military leaders to constantly give all their time and energy to the cause guaranteeing the rise of sociopaths whose only true loyalty is to themselves.

Every American needs to understand the true nature and motivations of its senior military leaders. Generals and Admirals do not necessarily deserve the hero worshiping sentiments of our citizens. These people have forfeited everything else in life to climb to the top. Unlike professional athletes and corporate executives who also travel extensively and dedicate extremely long hours to reach the pinnacle of performance, Generals and Admirals earn very modest wages (until they retire at least—more on this in the coming chapters) and

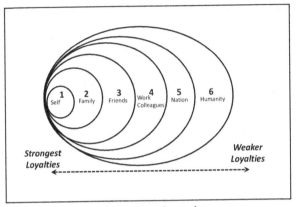

Figure 1: Loyalty Orbits

have almost no time for personal affairs. Military professionals cannot afford to bring their families with them wherever their travels might demand, and they spend years without seeing them at all when deployed abroad. Their families do not live in luxury insulated from the day-to-day struggles of most Americans so the excessive sacrifice must ring hollow for spouses and children. The average Flag officer today has deployed into combat zones for multiple years and has also "Geo-batched" for multiple years. Geo-batching requires an individual to take a short-term assignment in a new location while leaving his or her family behind to avoid disrupting their lives. In short, Flag officers make a conscious choice to tap out of being there for their families and friends for most of their professional lives spanning decades. These are the same people who make life and death decisions for America's sons and daughters in uniform. If they do not care enough about their own children to be there for them, however, do you think they really care about your children? Additionally, if career is everything, how much can we trust their testimony before Congress and the public regarding the progress of our wars? Have any of these leaders ever admitted defeat or delivered dark and ominous news? This is certainly not how one gets promoted. Naysayers are quickly culled from the uniformed leadership herd. Eighteen years into Afghanistan and the story from every military professional remains the same—we are making progress and remain on the verge of success. Many prominent Flag Officers run their mouths after retirement and speak out against various policies in an attempt to capture the spotlight, but where were their voices when they sat in positions of power? Did any of them oppose improper use of the military, wars to nowhere, enduring racism within the ranks, fraud, waste, or abuse? Crickets! A recent report from the Government Accountability Office, for instance, showed significant and enduring disparities in the military justice system along racial lines. Black service members are up to 71% more likely to receive administrative punishments and Courts Martial.[1] How dare any of these Generals who spent over three decades in uniform comment on race in America? They occupied positions to make change and did nothing. The problem lies squarely in the lap of the American public, however. We default to hero worshiping our senior uniformed

---

1 Dan Lamothe, *Military leaders promise to address systemic racial disparities in the military justice system*, The Washington Post, 16 June 2020.

leaders instead of asking tough questions and demanding tangible results.

America needs its heroes and heroines, but we must not misplace our affection and attention. Everyone in uniform does not equally deserve your adulation. We have serial killers, thieves, rapists, and sociopaths in our ranks as does any large organization. Real heroes and heroines do in fact exist, but contrary to the common notion, they do not necessarily fight for your freedom, Mom, and apple pie. They fight for each other and willingly accept the dangers associated with challenging circumstances to ensure their brothers and sisters in arms come home safely. The most noble sacrifices involve individuals putting their lives on the line for each other—not for you, me, or the mission. Our ranks are bursting at the seams with such individuals who are full of love for others. America should rightfully take pride knowing our country still produces so many such warriors. Unfortunately, these are not the same people who climb to the top of the military heap. As previously demonstrated, America's senior military leaders more often than not only love themselves and their careers. Perhaps when our young future heroes and heroines realize the corruption above them, the Department of Defense will be denied the cannon fodder it needs to perpetuate the routine and we will finally begin to get the changes we need.

Additionally, the state of constant warfare has unfortunately dumbed down the senior leadership of the Services. This condition preferentially selects individuals with a high enough pain threshold to endure the constant sacrifices necessary to lead in uniform but who possess limited talents to leverage in the civilian world. The US should put an end to the nepotism within its military leadership by appointing an independent entity to select Flag Officers based upon leader performance data not popularity with superiors and exposure to high level mentors. Justice for our Flag Officers also needs to be meted out by an independent commission to provide the transparency and accountability which does not exist today.

Many of the same forces which have given rise to unfit uniformed senior leadership exist across the entire spectrum of our society. Like a home with carpets soaked in cat urine, the funk of unfit leadership permeates every corner of American society. Look around and you will find the evidence everywhere. Corporate Executives who ride multi-million-dollar golden parachutes while their employees find themselves unemployed and pension-less. Elected officials who somehow accumulate wealth beyond imagination on relatively modest government salaries. Millionaires and billionaires who live within shouting distance of abject poverty but have never lifted a finger to help their fellow citizens. Approximately 90 billionaires call New York City home, for instance[2]. These

---

2 *Hillary Hoffower and Taylor Borden, Business Insider,* April 9, 2020,   https://www.businessinsider.com/where-do-billionaires-live-top-cities-worldwide-ranked-2019-5#1-new-york-city-is-the-worlds-only-city-with-more-than-90-billionaires-they-have-a-combined-net-worth-of-424-billion-10

same individuals hold the reins of power in both the private and public sectors—money is power. In the same city where these "leaders" accumulate more wealth than they could spend in a dozen lifetimes, untold thousands of children go to bed hungry every night and live in fear. A shameful but much too common example of a leadership crisis playing out across our nation.

This book is not about the pros and cons of various economic or political constructs, however. The situation is actually far simpler than abstract behavioral models and financial theories. Every problem can only survive in the absence of strong leadership. I learned this long ago as a cadet at West Point. The United States Military Academy trained me to think for myself and solve complex technical, organizational, and ethical dilemmas. Upon graduating and entering the commissioned officer ranks, however, I quickly learned to shelve my independent reasoning and morals in favor of unconditional obedience and loyalty to superiors in order to survive. These qualities serve as the coin of the public realm. The higher you climb, the more important they become. The following three decades of hands-on experience across a very diverse military and private sector career have further reinforced this unfortunate reality. Ask yourself why our nation bothers educating and training leaders of character if it ultimately rejects their principles in favor of wealth and influence? Maybe because a thriving democracy requires the illusion of worthy leadership if not the reality.

But deep in my heart, I know we desperately need inspired leaders who possess a positive vision, accept responsibility, hold others accountable, bring people together, and provide the resources to accomplish worthwhile objectives. End of discussion. You want to believe this as well. Leaders do not lay blame, lie, deny, make counteraccusations, pit individuals one against another, or simply ignore issues leaving them for their successors. The people we have placed in power, unfortunately, do not unanimously subscribe to these values. If they did, America would not have such an alarming host of problems which keep stacking up like cordwood. Back to fundamental reasoning—every problem is a leadership problem.

If you grow weary of the same old tired thinking regarding leadership and current affairs, this book is for you. Our country desperately needs fresh ideas so buckle up and prepare for a treasure-trove of unique and sometimes irreverent perspectives which will make you both laugh and squirm. Most importantly, I challenge the status quo with alternative ideas. I offer a journey with no punches pulled, no holds barred, and no dancing around delicate topics. These perspectives have grown from careful consideration of over thirty years in and around the military and its supporting businesses. Make no mistake, however, I am neither a hero nor a retired General. In the eyes of many, therefore, I lack a "platform", but this is exactly why you should keep reading. The types of people who climb to the top of the greasy pole of public leadership success think and act very much alike. Most are mere cookie-cutter silhouettes of conventional wisdom. In other words, if you have read one such volume from an authoritative big cheese, you have read them all. They succeeded under the current rules of the road so what could possibly need to change? In their minds, all you need to do to succeed is be more like them. Many are thinly veiled narcissists anyhow so why bother paying them homage? America must demand better!

Most of us, however, do not generally want to rock the boat because life is good for many people, especially for the middle and upper classes. We are wed to our collective prosperity. Furthermore, life is exceptionally good for the most wealthy and powerful in our ranks. What incentive do they have to champion meaningful change when they would likely risk losing their stranglehold on the status quo? Far easier to create a bullshit charade by pretending to champion reform. For the most part, those in charge seek to hypnotize the masses with the appearance of progress and equality while they draw more than a full measure off the fat of the land.

We must distinguish here between public and private sector leaders because they serve different masters. Cash is king in the private sector and profit motive most strongly incentivizes these leaders. Those who lead in the public domain, however, must serve a more noble master—the common good. Successful leaders in the private sector, therefore, do not necessarily have the requisite talents and personal attributes to serve the public. As a matter of fact, some private millionaires and billionaires garnered great wealth by taking advantage of people in a dog-eat-dog corporate ecosystem. Regardless of how effective they might be at running profit-making endeavors, such individuals have no "business" serving the public because they lack the proper motivations. When a billionaire, for instance, brags that he has not paid taxes in twenty years making him smarter than the rest of us, why do so many Americans not see him as a sociopath unfit for public office? If everyone were so "smart", both our society and government would collapse. No tax revenue, no government, no public assistance, no schools, no defense, etc.

If you too grow weary of seeing American greatness slowly rot on the vine, perhaps you are ready to tackle the really tough problems and consider alternative solutions. Read on and you will find fascinating perspectives and solutions to dysfunctional workplace behaviors, broken foreign policy approaches, persistent social injustice in America, wars to nowhere, and time management gone wrong. The first step to solving our problems is to acknowledge they exist—let us shatter the illusions!

Proposed Reforms

- Appoint an external governmental entity to oversee the promotion of Flag Officers based upon rigorous data and experiences not mere popularity with the entrenched Flags. Appropriate metrics are discussed in Chapter four.

- Empower civilian authority to prosecute Flag Officers. When any group of exceptionally ambitious people are entrusted to self-regulate, nepotism and corruption emerge. Hold Flag Officers criminally liable for providing false or misleading testimony regarding the progress of our wars and other military issues of great national importance.

CHAPTER 2

Systemic Racism is Dead

Sunlight is said to be the best of disinfectants.
Electric light, the best policeman.

—Louis Brandeis

I AM A 6' 5", 195-pound white male who never personally experienced discrimination. Learning to appreciate the issues surrounding racial injustice in the United States, therefore, has been an uphill, lifelong journey which never really ends. I grew up in a small farming community in upstate New York where 95% or more of the population remains Caucasian to this day. Nevertheless, I thought I knew the same hardships as young black people in America's inner cities and downtrodden communities. I had neither a father nor grandfather to help guide me and was raised by an uneducated single mother.

We drew welfare and food stamps when my mother was in-between jobs as a taxicab driver and factory worker who gapped spark plugs on an assembly line. I also knew what it meant to be chronically hungry. My physical development was probably delayed from malnourishment—I stood 4' 11" and 90 pounds as a freshman in high school. These hardships caused me to have little empathy for the plight of black people and other racial minorities as a young person. I felt as though my background made me just as disadvantaged as anyone else. At this young age, I still had much to learn, but a life of many and varied experiences has been an excellent teacher.

When I enlisted in the Army, my perspectives began to evolve. During basic training, roughly half my platoon consisted of people of color, mostly African Americans. The mutual challenges we suffered as basic trainees brought us close enough together to form trust and friendships. As we shared life experiences, I began to realize I was lucky to have been a white person who grew up in a rural community. Geography, environment, race, and socioeconomic status into which one is born all matter. Equal opportunity for everyone makes a nice bumper sticker, but simply does not hold true in America. For instance, I never had to worry about being harassed by the police solely because the color of my skin. Many of my fellow black soldiers struggled with this in their hometowns. Even though fatherless, blue collared men from farms, factories and small businesses surrounded me and provided ample positive role models. I did not have to struggle with violence, crime, drugs, and gangs at my doorstep. Yes, we were poor, but I knew what "right" looked like because of my environment. I thus began to understand for the first time the plight of African Americans suffering from generational poverty and systemic racism in dysfunctional neighborhoods. During this honeymoon period, however, I felt like the Army was an escape for people of all colors—a pure egalitarian system where we all had equal opportunity to move forward. From my foxhole, the Army was neither black, white, nor brown, it was green. I unconditionally loved the institution as well as my brothers and sisters in arms. Let the rest of America gnash its teeth about racism, but we were above such nonsense. Until we were not!

Shortly after arriving to my first unit in West Germany in 1987, I noticed cliques existed within my platoon along racial lines. Our discretionary time and freedom caused the differences between this unit and boot camp. In basic training, we were all frogs in the same pot of hot water learning to get along 24 x 7. In a regular unit, however, soldiers train and work together 10 to 14 hours a day but otherwise are free to do as they will. White guys explored Germany's cultural offerings in small groups as did African Americans and Latinos—three distinct groups had undoubtedly existed for decades. Everyone went to home base so to speak and hung out with people of the same skin color and cultural background. Further reinforcing this situation, many local clubs welcomed some types of people more than others. Conflict between soldiers occasionally erupted over competition for German women who were much more liberal and accepting of intra-racial relationships than most Americans in the 1980s. Few issues have the potential to cause more strife and tension than the competition for affection. There are no easy answers to these types of problems, and they persist today. As every new person in a military unit can attest, you end up gravitating towards the people who welcome you most. Other white soldiers quickly brought me into their fold by inviting me to join them in their off-duty pursuits. I never received an invitation from African American or Latino groups nor did us white guys ever invite minorities. Despite whom I chose to spend my free time with, however, I still felt like I did not have a racist bone in my body. We all just continued to operate within stovepipes. Sadly, this merely represents the illusion of full integration. America has yet to achieve a completely harmonious society where people freely socialize and form family ties across racial boundaries. In order to achieve the goal, we must eradicate the concept of African American, Latino, Caucasian, or Asian American neighborhoods in America.

When America looks at its uniformed formations and sees faces of all colors, it naturally draws the incorrect conclusion racism has been squelched in the military which has often been held up as the best example of full integration in our country. Contributing to this perception, the vast majority of Americans self-proclaim to be free from racial bias. Most, however, have a limited set of experiences which shape their perspectives. What can a powerful white male who was born a millionaire, never experienced prejudice, never struggled to find a job, never worked in the trenches so to speak and was never afraid to leave his house really understand about systemic racism in America? Far better for such a person to listen and appreciate the perspectives of those who have struggled than to tell them they simply need to pull themselves up by their bootstraps. Would Bill Gates, Warren Buffett or Donald Trump have risen to power if they were black men born into inner-city poverty? Highly unlikely in my opinion!

As my Army journey continued, I succeeded in a manner I had never before experienced in my life. Soldiering came naturally to such a strong extent that my chain of command from my squad leader up six levels to the very top noticed my performance and potential. My squad leader, platoon sergeant, platoon leader, company commander, battalion and regimental commanders all advocated for me to become a commissioned officer. Within a very fast paced year, therefore, I had a fully command endorsed application to the West Point preparatory school. This would never have occurred without support at all levels. Guess what race to which every single one of those leaders belonged? They were Caucasians just like me! I often look back and wonder if the outcome would have been the same if I were a young minority private. I honestly do not believe so.

I departed West Germany cutting my overseas tour short by entering West Point's five-year leadership pipeline. The total immersion in an extremely competitive academic, athletic, and professional military culture transformed me from an under-achieving poor white male into officer material. I emerged thinking, talking, and acting in accordance with the nation's finest military aristocratic traditions—pinky out! The cadets I graduated with in 1993 looked very much like America; racially proportionate but still predominantly male. The Corps of Cadets, however, is not very diverse from a socio-economic perspective. Regardless, of the race to which one belongs, the demanding West Point admissions criteria inadvertently screen out people who grew up low on the socioeconomic totem pole. A child who does not have a loving home with the resources to support multiple extracurricular activities and standardized test preparatory classes has almost no chance to gain admission. The same can be said of all prestigious American institutions. The people who most need to attend our nation's finest schools in order to break the cycle of generational poverty are the ones with the least chances given how we measure talent and aptitude. Nevertheless, on the surface, all appeared right with the world from an equal opportunity perspective. Until it was not!

After intensive infantry and ranger training, I arrived at the 82nd Airborne for duty as a rifle platoon leader within a battalion of 700 enlisted and 30 commissioned soldiers. Approximately half of my platoon of 40 paratroopers consisted of people of color which resonated with my previous enlisted experience on border patrol. Now that I was an officer, however, I had to put distance between myself and my soldiers. Fraternization, or getting too friendly with enlisted soldiers, remains forbidden. Further separating the ranks, my battalion commander routinely held officer professional development sessions or OPDs for short. These OPDs required gathering only the commissioned officers together in a small forum to participate in team building and advanced educational opportunities (ask yourself if the distinction between enlisted and officer ranks is still necessary or if it is an anachronism from the days of royalty). We often met at the Fort Bragg officers' club and followed the formal activities with drinks, war stories and camaraderie late into the evening. At this first session, I immediately noticed how white we were as a group. There was not a single commissioned officer of color in our group, yet we led soldiers who were incredibly diverse. How does this happen I wondered? West Point and all other commissioning sources such as the Reserve Officer Training Corps or ROTC take great pains to graduate people of all ethnicities as a representative cross-section of America. New officers, however, get a vote when choosing their job specialties and locations. Why would minority commissioned officers not want to serve in the renowned 82nd Airborne Division as infantry officers? After all, the path to becoming a General begins and ends with service in the Army's elite combat divisions of which there are only two types: infantry and armor. The answer to the conundrum is obvious. The senior leadership of these prestigious units continues to be dominated by white males even to this day. Minority officers, therefore, tend to seek service in other units where they feel they have a better chance to succeed. Helen Cooper points out how extensively white senior military leadership remains within the Trump administration.[3] The nation's efforts over the last 75 years to fully integrate the military and promote diversity have obviously failed yet we cling to the notion the military looks like the nation it represents from top to bottom. It does not. The same can be said for all other major institutions in America. Implementing quotas to ensure minority representation on the team falls short of the ultimate goal. I put myself in the boots of a young black private in my infantry battalion. Looking around at the exclusively white male commissioned officers, I certainly would not have felt like I had the same chance to succeed as Caucasian peers. If it looks like a white man's world, it probably is. People of all backgrounds must proportionally rise to the very top if we are to achieve lasting peace and harmony. At first glance, it appears all military personnel have equal opportunity, but the end results do not substantiate this claim. The fact that young black officers deliberately avoid many of the most successful career fields condemns the Army on two levels—both process and people. Minorities have little faith that there are processes in place to ensure the career playing field is equal. They are also leery of working for senior white officers who can prevent their rise through a completely subjective evaluation system.

---

3 Helene Cooper, *African Americans Are Highly Visible in the Military but almost Invisible at the Top* (New York Times, 25 May, 2020).

This first OPD experience sparked a lifelong interest in learning more about the problem of race in our country. We have lots of dirty secrets which we do not teach our young people. For instance, the very first settlers at Jamestown brought 20 African slaves with them in 1619. Two hundred and thirty-five years later, this population had soared to an astonishing four million at the height of the American Civil War.[4] Imagine the fortunes made on the backs of so many enslaved people who toiled their entire lives with no hope of a better future and no compensation. Are you naïve enough to believe these fortunes no longer exist? Much like generational poverty, generational wealth also lives on. Most Americans readily recognize the Ford, Rockefeller, Carnegie, and Pullman names for instance because the wealth and influence earned by previous generations ends up in enduring family trusts. None of the incredible resources reaped from slavery, however, were ever used to help the emancipated yet these monies most assuredly have grown and still exist today. Our nation took precious little action at the conclusion of the Civil War to welcome freed slaves into our society and economy. Imagine the plight of these four million people who had no money, little education, no family ties beyond the confines of their former plantations and were largely unwelcome in most communities. Some stayed in the South and continued to work the same lands as share-croppers—indentured servants

---

4 Ernie Suggs, *1619 The First Africans arrive in the New World* (The Atlanta Journal Constitution, February 7, 2017).

by any other name. Others fled to urban centers in the North and Mid-west seeking wage labor where they attained the work no one else wanted.

Hatred and resentment for the freed slaves quickly erupted as their influence and presence spread across the country. A group of former Confederate veterans formed the Ku Klux Klan in 1865 in Tennessee and elected former Confederate General Nathan Bedford Forest as its first grand wizard.[5] They established an "Invisible Empire of the South" violently targeting African Americans and politicians who supported liberal reconstruction policies aimed at bringing former slaves into the economic fold. Incredibly, at its height in 1920, the KKK had over four million members. Quite shockingly, the KKK claimed 11 state Governors, 16 Senators, and 75 Congressman as members during this timeframe![6] In places where African Americans began to succeed, white supremacy emerged with political backing to violently put them back in their place. The Tulsa, Oklahoma race massacre in 1921 which left hundreds of blacks dead and 1000 of their homes burned to the ground provides an excellent example.[7] The

5 History.com Editors, *Ku Klux Kan* (https://www.history.com/topics/reconstruction/ku-klux-klan 21 February 2020).
6 Jon Meacham, *The Soul of America, The Battle For Our Better Angels*, page 111, Random House, 2018.
7 Alexis Clark, *Tulsa's Black Wall Street Flourished as a Self-Contained Hub in early 1900s* (https://www.history.com/news/black-wall-street-tulsa-race-massacre, 2 January 2020)

riot touched off when an African American allegedly raped a Caucasian woman. With no other evidence than hearsay and no trial, the white community violently attacked its black neighbors. Further stoking Caucasian rage, the African American sub-community of Greenwood was incredibly wealthy and prosperous. Jealousy obviously played a role in the massacre. Sadly, Greenwood never recovered its former glory after these attacks, and no one was ever held accountable. This is just one such example of many ugly counter-reactions to rising African American influence in American history. Further consider the alarming political influence of white supremacy in the 1920s sixty years after emancipation. Much like wealth and poverty, political power is also generational. The families of those aforementioned Governors, Senators and Congressmen who marched with the KKK most assuredly continue to wield influence today.

The table had thus been set for generational poverty and continued exploitation of African Americans. In the last 150 years, nothing meaningful has changed despite the apparent efforts of leaders of all races and walks of life. While the Civil Rights Act of 1964 ended the morally repugnant Jim Crow laws in the South, our nation still has done nothing to address the issue of generational poverty in African American communities. Well-meaning public entitlement programs such as welfare and food stamps only serve as a Band-Aid on the sucking chest wound of poor and dysfunctional communities. When first passed into law in 1964, the Food Stamp Act provided much needed nutrition assistance to low income households. Black people in particular were literally starving in droves across our nation in places like the Mississippi River delta. No one should go hungry in such a prosperous nation. Fast forward to today, however, and these same communities remain downtrodden while people kill themselves one spoonful at a time. Obesity, diabetes, and heart disease have largely replaced starvation. Within our inner cities, the "Projects" provided subsidized housing for destitute peoples, but we never moved past these transient efforts. Many such housing centers have transformed into dysfunctional communities crippled with violence and crime. These tragic reversals of fortune have resulted from our failures to address the root causes of disenfranchised communities one of which remains systemic racism.

The black vote sadly remains a political football. One end of the spectrum clings to the idea that slavery ended 155 years ago, and African Americans need to just get over it. The other end wants to dole out a never-ending series of apologies and entitlements in exchange for votes. Neither intends to actually address the very real and lingering detrimental impacts of slavery as their political fortunes remain tied to the status quo. What has changed in inner-city Chicago, New York, or Los Angles since 1964? One ugly answer—an explosion in the trafficking of illegal drugs and the rise of gangs who fight for influence. Inner-city African Americans and other disenfranchised people now serve as pawns on the big money chessboard of drug cartels and intermediate distributors. Downtrodden people consume and market the product for higher level wealthy factions who care only about money and power and not the consequences of their business. Our elected leaders do nothing about this crisis. Why? How many politicians today secretly serve in the KKK or other extremist groups? No better way to keep African Americans enslaved than to put food in their bellies with handouts and drugs in their bodies to dull the senses. Entire communities unwittingly become sheep to be sheared by a different kind of master who has burrowed deep underground. As demonstrated by the widespread outcry in response to the murder of George Floyd, public brutality draws far too much attention in the modern era. Perhaps the new goal of the most powerful and cunning white supremacy groups is covertly promoting generational poverty and systemic racism while pretending to have noble objectives. These are not the hateful idiots we see in public demonstrations. The most dangerous enemy is the one who befriends you under false pretenses while working to undermine your every move. Where are the leaders willing to stop pussyfooting around and address these issues?

Fast forward several years past my first OPD at Fort Bragg, and my command nominated me to compete for a prestigious leadership award. In order to increase my visibility (Impression and Exposure), I was placed on a small panel of officers who were selected for their maturity and potential to serve at a higher level. We collectively decided the fate of all military personnel considered for administrative separation across our installation of over 25,000 military members. Such cases require a keen sense of justice because we had the power to recommend involuntarily removing people from the service while leaving the soldier no other recourse. Most candidates brought before the board demonstrated a pattern of misconduct while failing to respond to lower-level corrective actions such as negative evaluations, reduction in rank, forfeiture of pay and after-hours extra duty. Administrative separation was a measure of last resort within the military justice system.

Along came a case involving a Latino Sergeant First Class who used the "N word" in the installation's military housing area. I will refer to him as Sergeant X. One evening after dinner, Sergeant X's ten-year-old son burst through the doors of his quarters holding a bloody head wound. His son told him that a neighbor had smashed him in the head with a bat. Sergeant X flew out of the house in anger and with the help of his son found the perpetrator who was a young African American boy. Sergeant X marched the assailant to his parents' house and knocked on the door. When the assailant's father who was also a soldier answered, Sergeant X angrily explained what had happened and told the father he needed to keep his little "N" boy under control. He then marched back to his quarters and considered the matter closed. The African American family rightfully took great offense to the slander and reported the event to Sergeant X's commander. Sergeant X had 19 years of service and this was the first negative incident in his official record. Sergeant X's commander could have taken a host of other actions as previously mentioned and even could have had his subordinate very appropriately kicked out of government housing. Unfortunately for Sergeant X, news of the event quickly traveled all the way up the chain of command to a high level General. The General wanted Sergeant X referred for administrative separation, so the company commander quickly complied even though the decision lay squarely in his lap not the General's.

When the case hit the panel and we heard all the details, I derailed the proceedings by insisting the punishment did not fit the crime. Sergeant X was less than a year away from retirement representing a pension of approximately $40,000 per year and free health care for the rest of his life. Administration separation would have denied him all these benefits and resulted in an "other than honorable" discharge. In effect, the punishment exceeded a million-dollar fine and would seriously damage SFC X's future employment prospects. This felt excessively heavy-handed to me. Furthermore, imagine SFC X's reaction to the punishment. Having been around the block a time or two, I knew when people feel like they have nothing left to lose, they become a danger to themselves and others. SFC X would still have to look his African American neighbors in the eyes as he moved out of government quarters with his life in complete shambles. No justice, no peace. I began to convince other members of the board to side with me. At this point, the chief legal counsel assigned to the board pulled me aside and privately let me know I was on thin ice. This case was important to the General. Why was it so important to him I wondered? Was this Caucasian male General interested in ensuring we did the right thing or making a name for himself as a uniformed civil rights advocate? Additionally, I began to feel like I had been appointed to a kangaroo court established to simply do the bidding of higher authority while presenting the illusion of due process. As already discussed in great detail, most everyone in a position of power constantly seeks the next promotion. Those who sacrifice everything to climb to the top too often put moral and ethical considerations on the back burner. My heart told me that Sergeant X was a sacrificial lamb for the General's future advancement. If we are to avoid a negative counter-reaction to civil rights issues, we must not over-react with excessively harsh punishments. We must also beware of the ulterior motives of leaders who seek to garner fame and attention by simply looking tough without true interest in reform.

Selective acceptable usage of the "N" word highlights the existence of a double standard. People of color use it all the time and it routinely emerges in music and pop culture. As a white male, however, I know I should NEVER use it and further understand the importance of intent. African Americans sometimes use it as a term of affection and brotherhood. Sergeant X on the other hand clearly used it in a hateful manner and deserved punishment. This distinction matters and must be acknowledged. Not every non-African American, however, is so enlightened. In the best possible future world, we would all equally avoid using the term.

Other double standards include the acknowledgement that African Americans are on average stronger, faster, and more athletic, than Caucasians. Additionally, many contend that Asian Americans make the best and hardest working students—especially in math and science. As far as I know, no one but white supremacist groups in the modern era contend Caucasians are more gifted in any particular domain than any other race. None of these stereotypes bother me because I am comfortable in my own skin. Again, not every Caucasian is so enlightened. I suppose it is the curse of the racial majority as well as our ugly national history which have resulted in this sad state of affairs. Nevertheless, we should all work to remove them from our speech and thinking. Stereotypes can lead to prejudice and prejudice is a circular track of perpetual hatred.

Recent and prominent examples of police brutality aimed at African Americans provide more evidence of ongoing systemic racism in America. We will discuss these further in the coming chapters within the framework of leadership accountability failures. Individual police officers who use unnecessary violence, their negligent supervisors, and District Attorneys who look the other way must be held criminally liable for both their actions and their inaction. A lack of accountability rightfully drives the Black Lives Matter movement and there will be no peace until we resolve these injustices.

Sadly, many of my Caucasian colleagues insist systemic racism is dead. I would love to believe this as well, but unfortunately, my eyes are wide open, and I refuse to deny the evidence which keeps popping up. Take the case of retired US Navy Captain Scott Bethmann and his wife Nancy. Captain Bethmann climbed to a revered position in the Navy and commanded sailors of all ethnic backgrounds for over two decades. Upon retirement, he assumed a prestigious role within the Naval Academy's alumni association. Surely a closet racist could not effectively hide his true sentiments for so long could he? Unfortunately for the Captain, he and his wife inadvertently live-streamed a hateful racist dialogue for 30 minutes on Facebook commenting on the response to the national reaction to George Floyd's murder.[8] Captain Bethmann's subsequent apology rings hollow. He is probably only mortified because his true feelings finally surfaced likely ruining any further career prospects. People say what they really feel in the privacy of their homes. Unfortunately for all of us, this example vividly demonstrates the stain of systemic racism lives on and must be addressed with open minds and hearts. People of all walks too often speak their opinions which may or may not be well-informed without truly listening to others with opposing views.

The African American community does not stand alone as victims of systemic racism. Consider the plight of Native

---

8 Yaron Steinbuch, *Retired Navy captain apologizes after livestreaming racial slurs on Facebook* (New York Post, June 8, 2020).

Americans who once occupied the entire continent and now reside within the narrow confines of some of the nation's most marginal lands. These people continue to suffer from generational poverty and lack of access to quality education and career opportunities, and nobody really seems to care. Illegal aliens from Central America, on the other hand, come to the United States freely, but we subsequently take advantage of them. They take the hard labor jobs few other people desire and do so for far less than fair market value. This increases the profit margin of many businesses and results in lower costs for consumer goods and services. Additionally, politicians use them by promising to ignore their illegal status in return for their votes. America thus has neither a financial nor a political incentive to stop exploiting them.

Simply continuing on with the status quo which has not yielded the desperately needed results is no longer acceptable. Repeatedly doing the same thing and expecting a different result is the epitome of stupidity. I offer the measures below for consideration as new and different ways to tackle the problem:

Proposed Reforms

- Augment racial quotas with targeted access to career fast-track opportunities for minorities to ensure representation at the highest levels. People will never feel like the system is fair until they see leaders of all types rise to the very top in the military, politics, business, arts, and entertainment.

- Commission a study by an independent government entity such as the Government Accountability Office (GAO) to trace the fortunes made from slavery. Find and tax these to provide enhanced educational and housing opportunities for African Americans. In short, use these resources to begin to address the root causes and effects of systemic racism in the US.

- Label all racial supremacist groups as terrorist organizations and mobilize the full resources of the US military, intelligence, and investigative arms to expose them and confiscate their resources.

- Police Officers must be held criminally liable for their brutal actions. Others in leadership positions who ignore crimes or use their discretion to keep cases from going to court should be charged with obstruction of justice.

- Legalize all drug trade and place the manufacture, distribution, and ultimate sale in the hands of the nation's thriving gang structure. In short, recruit the radicals and transform enemies into allies by making them legitimate businesspeople. By decriminalizing these activities, we can begin to establish a thriving taxable economy which will profit the inner-city poor and oppressed. The current war on drugs is an illusion perpetuated by the ultra-wealthy benefactors anyhow. Consider the case of deaths due to opioid addiction which have quadrupled since 1999. Most of these deaths until 2015 were from legally prescribed sources which have only recently been surpassed by heroin and synthetic sources.[9] Big pharmaceuticals in the US made billions of dollars from drugs such as oxycodone so a death every 16 minutes from overdose must have been acceptable collateral damage. Politicians are only now getting more serious about the problem because the money is shifting into hands which do not offer campaign contributions. Decriminalizing all drugs would leverage the leadership of young people of all racial backgrounds already immersed in the drug trade and dramatically decrease police tension across the nation.

---

9 Center for Disease Control, "Opioid Overdose, understanding the epidemic", https://www.cdc.gov/drugoverdose/epidemic/index.html

CHAPTER 3

Wars keep us Safe

This conjunction of an immense military establishment and a large arms industry is new in the American experience. We recognize the imperative need for this development [but]...we must not fail to comprehend its grave implications. We must guard against the acquisition of unwarranted influence...the potential for the disastrous rise of misplaced power exists and will persist.

—President Dwight D. Eisenhower's farewell address, January 17, 1961

A S A YOUNG MAN, I had a very idealistic concept of warfare. This vision resulted from the historical perspective of American fighting men and women driving the British from the North American continent, smashing the tyrannical Nazi and Imperial Japanese war machines, and preventing communism from sweeping across the globe. I watched the Viet Nam war on television in the days when we only had three channels from which to choose and made up my mind what I wanted to be when I grew up. I enlisted in the Army at age 19 and retired thirty years later as a 49-year-old in search of a new career. I willingly gave my best years to the service. Soldiers from the rank and file will always be my heroes and heroines. While the United States has used its unprecedented military might as a force for good for the most part, my many years around the military have transformed my views. The true nature of war is abhorrent and remains unchanged from primitive times despite the trappings of modern civilization. If anything, warfare has taken on a far uglier mask as we find more efficient and less personal ways to kill each other. We routinely bring widespread death and destruction without ever looking anyone in the eyes. In order to avoid unnecessary wars, we must first understand the powerful forces which drive us to this tragic state of affairs.

The devil himself must have minted the first coin in the forges of Hell and we have fought over it since. Satan, if you chose to believe he exists, surely considers the concept of money his greatest invention since original sin. A shiny gold doubloon probably sits atop his mantle alongside an apple. On the high end of the economic spectrum, money allows people to accumulate vastly more goods and services than either they or their entire family could consume in a dozen lifetimes thus encouraging the sins of gluttony and greed. On the low end, people murder each other every day for the resources required to merely survive.

The deadliest manifestation of the evil money promotes is full-blown armed conflict in which rival factions use every means available to destroy each other and claim resources. The British, for instance, committed significant military power to prevent the American colonies from achieving independence. The crown stood to lose tax revenues and access to the bounty of the North American continent for which it was willing to fight. The Nazi regime launched World War II largely for "Lebensraum", a massive land grab to attain the territory necessary to achieve economic and political dominion over Europe. You get the idea—war in every era revolves around resources. In order to fully understand why the United States (US) is now mired in its longest conflict (18 years and counting engaged in the Global War on Terror (GWOT)), therefore, we need only follow the money.

Since 9/11 through the end of 2020, the US has committed to spending approximately 6.4 trillion dollars on counter-terrorism efforts while prosecuting the GWOT.[10] This huge sum poses a challenge for many people to fully comprehend. One way of placing it in perspective is to compare it to total Federal spending for a year. In 2019, the US Government

---

10 *Costs of War Project*, Watson Institute for International and Public Affairs, Brown University. https://watson.brown.edu/costsofwar/about

planned to spend approximately $4.5 trillion on all activities.[11] This funds both discretionary (Defense, Energy, Department of State, NASA, Health and Human Services, Education, etc.) and non-discretionary requirements (Social Security, Medicare, Medicaid, Affordable Care Act, Federal Pensions, Interest on the debt, etc.). Congress can only avoid non-discretionary spending by passing new legislation. Discretionary spending, therefore, provides the only realistic trade space to adjust Federal spending of which defense is the dominant variable. Putting the $6.4 trillion in context then, we have spent as much chasing terrorists in 18 years as we will spend on all other federal programs in the next 18 months. Would we be willing to halt all Federal activities and payments to include Social Security, Medicare, and Medicaid for such a long period to fund fighting terrorists abroad? On a per capita basis, every man, woman, and child in the US would have to pay $19,394 to fully fund what our Government has already spent on GWOT to date and there is no end in sight (based on a population in 2020 of 330 million).

The table below presents a detailed breakdown of discretionary costs. Consider the relative benefits of war versus laying the groundwork for future success. As seen below, the Federal Government spends more than 10 times as much annually on

---

11 Office of Management and Budget. https://www.thebalance.com/fy-2019-federal-budget-summary-of-revenue-and-spending-4589082

Defense as it does on education. While detailed records do not exist, it is probable that we have spent more on the GWOT in the past 18 years than we have spent on education in the entire history of our country! Ask yourself if we the people have received a good return on our investment.

Table 1 (US Discretionary Spending in 2019)

Department	President's Request in 2019 (Billions)
Defense	$686
Health and Human Services	$70
Education	$59.9
Veteran's Affairs	$83.1
Homeland Security	$52.7
Energy	$29.2
Housing and Urban Development	$29.2
State Department	$40.3
NASA	$19.9
All Others	$133.1
TOTAL	**$1305**

While nobody likes to put a price on human life, consider the case of a military service member killed in combat. The Department of Defense provides a death gratuity of a mere $100,000 to the benefactors of the deceased.[12] This meager sum

---

12 Military pay and compensation. https://militarypay.defense.gov/ Benefits/Death-Gratuity/

reaffirms the old adage "life is cheap" and also anchors the logic of government spending. If we are willing to allocate such huge sums on war, both in blood and treasure, we must ask ourselves what we have gained? How much safer are we? How many American lives have been spared by fighting terrorism abroad? If a US soldier, airman or marine is only worth $100,000 to our government, then the GWOT would only be a reasonable financial investment if we saved 64 million American lives (64 Million x $100,000 = $6.4 trillion: the cost of GWOT to date). This callous, emotionally bankrupt calculation demonstrates that our safety and security are not priceless. Forfeiting so much blood and treasure to beat back both real and imagined terrorists at our gates does not make good financial sense. We are on the wrong side of the cost curve.

Nevertheless, the world continues to shrink making resource competition fiercer than ever, the ultimate cause of most wars. The foreign policy makers, politicians, and military planners of the US, however, have lost sight of the essential economic nature of conflict. The focus has shifted to upholding moral principles, overthrowing corrupt regimes, and spreading democracy, but every dollar we spend on these endeavors is a dollar not spent on other priorities. We have boots on the ground in over 140 nations across the globe at great cost, but few leaders or citizens question how this advances our long-term economic interests. Where are the leaders willing to ask if the juice is worth the squeeze? Many contend the massive force projection keeps us safer at home—better to fight terrorists on their turf than on the streets of our cities. If we examine the root causes of terrorism against the US, however, this argument quickly disintegrates.

Anyone willing to give their life to kill innocent civilians is filled with hatred and herein lies the source of the ailment: hatred against the US and our way of life. Tragically, the US strategy of active military engagement likely only further stokes these flames. After nearly 20 years of combat operations, we have killed hundreds of thousands of people, many of whom were non-combatant, innocent bystanders, displaced millions due to the lack of security in their homelands and emplaced largely unwelcome western cultural institutions. The following staggering figures outline some of the costs of war we have inflicted upon our "enemies":[13]

- Over 801,000 deaths due to direct war violence
- 335,000 civilians have been killed
- 21 Million war refugees and displaced persons

Doubtful that all of the survivors of the chaos we have induced in Iraq, Afghanistan, Syria and elsewhere have come to love us. The US has thus created the world's most dangerous self-licking ice cream cone. We must continue to chase terrorists across the globe because the process of doing so spawns a never-ending supply of radical recruits. We need only recall how our ancestors responded to foreign soldiers living amongst

---

13 "Costs of War", Watson Institute for International & Public Affairs, Brown University.

American colonists. The active British and mercenary military presence fomented hatred and resentment which provided George Washington with thousands of new volunteers. Have we forgotten our history?

Additionally, our current extensive military campaigns contribute to a very dangerous national debt which may one day topple our very way of life. The kabuki dance continues because war lines the pockets of the winners of defense contracts who cleverly contribute heavily to political campaigns. Our elected officials subsequently control which General Officers and Admirals rise through the ranks and as one might guess, naysayers do not fare well. Allowing four-star military personnel and former defense industry executives to make war policy decisions is akin to putting the Cookie-monster in charge of the bakery. Upon retirement, these same Flag officers find themselves in cozy defense industry senior leadership positions with bloated compensation packages as a reward for their "service". As previously discussed, these retired Generals selected their replacements for promotion and therefore have access to their loyal former subordinates. On any given day, a host of retired Flag Officers who now work for Defense industry parade through the Pentagon's corridors gripping and grinning. Their new employers count on the retired Flag Officer's rolodexes to get them access to senior officials who can influence multi-billion-dollar contract awards. If you believe in capitalism, these retired Flags only merit huge salaries if they actually can influence contract award. They have nothing else to offer private corporations which make their money building weapons. I suppose these officers fool themselves into believing they add value to defense industry in order to sleep at night. At the highest levels, the military has sadly degenerated into organized corruption hiding in plain sight. Defense industry, politicians who accept their generous contributions, and senior military personnel, therefore, have monopolized the policy making and execution arms of warfare in the US. There is no room on the bus for doves. War is good for business, big money influences representatives whom in turn guarantee the rise of military officers supporting the hawkish agenda. This war really is about economics, but only politicians, senior officers and defense industry partners ultimately benefit. As an example, the current Secretary of Defense in 2020 formerly served as the Vice President for Government Relations at the Raytheon Company (a Defense Contracting giant).[14] The Secretary of the Army rose to his position along a similar trajectory having previously served as a Vice President for Lockheed Martin.[15] Their official biographies unabashedly highlight these defense industry positions as somehow making them more qualified to provide civilian oversight of the mechanisms of war. Both these gentlemen earned significant sums from winning and managing defense contracts for their parent corporations. They now sit

---

14 Official Biography, Mark T. Esper. https://www.defense.gov/Our-Story/Biographies/Biography/Article/1378166/dr-mark-t-esper/
15 Official Biography, Ryan D. McCarthy. https://www.army.mil/leaders/sa/bio/

in the ultimate power positions to influence the course of our wars. Curtailing US involvement would mean lower profits for their former colleagues, yet we allow this blatant conflict of interest to continue because most regular citizens have no idea. Meanwhile, the American people tacitly support the conflicts because fear mongers of many kinds continue to fan the flames of paranoia and xenophobia.

Enter two new antagonists: Russia and China. While the US focused exclusively on terrorism, these two competitors emerged from the shadows with capabilities to threaten our military dominance. The 2018 US National Defense Strategy (NDS), therefore, calls for modernized weapons and doctrine to contain these nations.[16] Call it Cold War 2.0—rebooted from the 1945 through 1991 era. Regardless of the perceived necessity of these efforts, who really believes we can afford them? As discussed above, we have already bled the treasury dry and incurred lasting debts which will linger for generations. It does not matter what we the people believe, however. As Americans finally grow tired of the GWOT, those who benefit from war will create new threats to justify the huge expenditures which line their pockets.

Nevertheless, if we review global affairs since the end of World War II, several important developments have emerged

---

16 Summary of the 2018 National Defense Strategy. https://dod. defense.gov/Portals/1/Documents/pubs/2018-National-Defense-Strategy-Summary.pdf

which make the reoccurrence of high-intensity conflict with other great powers highly improbable. The extensive nuclear arsenals of Russia, China, and the United States (among others) prevent a conventional slug fest because Mutually Assured Destruction or MAD for short is still a thing. The 45 year-long Cold War with the Soviet Union, for instance, never went hot, and this should teach us something. Great powers in the nuclear era behave rationally; they do not seek to end civilization and thus avoid open and catastrophic conflict with peers. So why should we borrow hundreds of billions of dollars from our children to build weapons that will likely never be used? Recall the Soviet Union spent itself into oblivion in an arms race with the US it could not win while also waging a discretionary war of attrition in Afghanistan. The US defeated the Soviet Union without ever firing a shot—economic dominance prevailed. Two key takeaways: 1) It is both possible and preferable in the modern era to achieve national objectives against peer adversaries via non-violent means, and 2) The US now finds itself in the exact position as the Soviet Union in 1990 on the eve of collapse; militarily over-extended while struggling to spend ever more on defense to counter peer adversaries.

Great power competition endures, but it has taken on a new mask in an ever broader and more interconnected global community. The struggle is almost entirely economic; powerful nations race to secure the markets and natural resources required to remain economically vibrant. Consider Africa for a moment, the most under-developed, habitable corner of the Earth remaining. US Special Forces comb the continent in search of terrorists while our foreign policy makers resist supporting African leaders with questionable ethics and human rights records. We bring death and the threat of regime change—one of our favorite and internationally least popular tools. The Chinese on the other hand usher in development, business, jobs, and prosperity with no moral strings attached. Note this clever strategy requires absolutely no military spending and provides new jobs and markets. The Chinese understand the economics of power struggle; they play chess while we play checkers.

Meanwhile, our competitors benefit from the stability provided by widespread US engagement and simply wait for us to exhaust our blood and treasure. These same antagonists have stolen our intellectual crown jewels and developed capabilities to bring our economy to a screeching halt without ever firing a shot. They have no intention of fighting bloody, high-intensity battles with the US. No need to accept this risk when they can instead simply watch the US impale itself upon our greed and outdated approaches to warfare and international affairs. But it is not too late for the US to recognize the economic nature of the ongoing competition and take appropriate action. We merely need a Congress willing to balance the books and defense planners able to redesign the National Defense Strategy from square one. Collin Powell, former Chairman of the Joint Chiefs of Staff and Secretary of State, famously outlined eight yes or no questions which should be answered in the affirmative before waging war.[17] Applying Powell's deliberate logic and thought process by no means presents a compelling case for the wars in Iraq, Afghanistan, Syria and elsewhere which continue to linger.

1. **Is a vital national security interest threatened? YES**
   (Terrorist training camps and enclaves persist in many places around the world. These groups continue to plan to harm the US and our interests abroad.)

2. **Do we have a clear attainable objective? NO**
   (Stopping people from planning criminal activity in every corner of the world is impossible. Coining the term "terrorism" and applying it to global criminal activity does not magically transform it into something which can be conquered with tanks, planes, and machineguns. We cannot even stop domestic terrorists and extremists within the borders of the US. Why should we believe we can stop it in hostile lands which oppose our very presence? Additionally, consider the moral complexity of pre-emptively killing terrorists. Many attend training camps with the intent to perhaps one day do us harm, but as of yet, have never lifted a finger against the US. Killing them is tantamount to executing a US citizen

---

17 Stephen M. Walt, "Applying the eight questions of the Powell doctrine to Syria", September 3, 2013. https://foreignpolicy. com/2013/09/03/applying-the-8-questions-of-the-powell-doctrine-to-syria/

who planned a murder but never carried out the deed. What if the would-be perpetrator changes their mind or can never reach the US to carry out a mission? Other terrorists include children who unknowingly ride bicycles with the internal tubes packed with explosives into crowds of US soldiers. These bicycles can be remotely detonated by an evil puppet master. What are the US soldiers to do given such ugly cases? Shoot all kids on bicycles who come anywhere near US forces? These are real problems we face every day.)

3. **Have the risks and costs been fully and frankly analyzed? NO**

(Very little public discussion or debate regarding the risks and costs. Pussyfooted politicians of all parties continue to support the wars because doing nothing threatens their images—they might look unpatriotic or, worse yet, be blamed for another terrorist attack. They would also risk losing campaign contributions from defense industry. War with no bounds comes with other very ugly costs aside from combat casualties. The Department of Veteran Affairs reported in 2019 at least 60,000 Veterans have committed suicide from 2008 to 2017.[18] These suicides are a directly correlated

---

18 "2019 Veteran National Suicide Annual Prevention Report", Office of Mental Health and Suicide Prevention, US Office of Veteran's Affairs, page 3.

cost of prosecuting morally problematic, complex and never-ending wars. Placing this terrible number in perspective, Veteran suicides in the last 10 years alone exceed all combat fatalities during the 14 years of the Viet Nam Conflict and currently average approximately 20 per day. This is approximately one veteran suicide every 85 minutes, 24 hours a day, 365 days a year. As Mike Hayne writes "The final casualty of the Viet Nam War was not the elimination of the draft. Instead it was, by eliminating the draft in favor of a volunteer military, to disconnect the costs and consequences of war from the overwhelming majority of Americans."[19])

4. **Have all other nonviolent policy means been fully exhausted? NO**

(In the aftermath of 9/11, the US sought vengeance, not long-term solutions. No amount of military force will stop future terrorists from attending flight school in the US and plotting to fly civilian aircraft into our landmarks. More restrictive immigration policies, thorough vetting of military and civilian trainees in the US, and a laissez-faire foreign policy approach in the Middle East will do far more to prevent future attacks

---

19 Mike Haynie, "Why the epidemic of veteran suicide?", Syracuse University Institute for Veterans and Military families. https://www.syracuse.com/opinion/2019/11/why-the-epidemic-of-veteran-suicide-because-it-aint-me-commentary.html

than military force. The US relationship with Iran, for instance, has been forever poisoned by the CIA's efforts to install a pro-US regime under the Shah. As a reward for our meddling, the Shah gave US oil companies a 40% share in Iran's oil fields.[20] Are you beginning to see how our wars really do revolve around money? Iranian revolutionaries under Ayatollah Khomeini, however, overthrew the Shah (the US guy in Iran) in 1979, took American hostages, and implemented anti-American policies. Iran continues to fund terrorist activities against the US today—our reward for attempting to influence the internal politics of other nations. Yet we continue to try to pick the winners and losers in Afghanistan, Iraq, and Syria to name a few.)

5. **Is there a plausible exit strategy to avoid endless entanglement? NO**

(No politician or military professional has yet to define success. Overthrowing regimes in Iraq, Afghanistan, and Syria, for instance, does not provide a firm end to hostilities. A new regime must fill the void and there are no guarantees it will be any better. Implementing democracy in a population which hates Americans will de facto result in a new anti-US government.

20 "CIA assisted coup overthrows government of Iran", This Day in History, August 15, 2019. https://www.history.com/this-day-in-history/cia-assisted-coup-overthrows-government-of-iran

Additionally, the remnants of any ousted faction will go into hiding and continue to resist. A war waged by outsiders attempting to determine the governing faction in a foreign land, therefore, knows no end. The US Army recently adopted a "winning matters" slogan in an effort to counter rising pacifist sentiments. The institution fails to see the tragically ridiculous irony in that statement. What exactly does winning mean in our current wars? Nobody in either the military or political establishments has defined this yet so we will continue to run with scissors.)

6. **Have the consequences of our action been fully considered? NO**

   (We continue to reap the secondary and tertiary implications of long-term military occupation of foreign lands. These were never discussed prior to invading Iraq, Afghanistan, and Syria. The casualties and chaos we have inflicted upon our enemies and innocent civilian bystanders caught up in the violence have created an endless conveyor belt of radical recruits. Southwest Asia largely rejects Western culture with the exception of Israel.)

7. **Is the action supported by the American people? MIXED**

   (This depends upon who you ask. Both political parties support the war leaving the American people with no pro-peace alternatives at the ballot box.)

8. Do we have genuine broad international support? MIXED

(Again, it depends upon who you ask. NATO partners continue to send military forces to Afghanistan, but their contributions are very small in comparison to the US presence. NATO is only a fraction of the international community. Russia, for instance, actively opposes US efforts in Syria. China, India, Japan, and Brazil remain aloof.)

When we combine numbers two and five above, our government and military have yet to define either an attainable goal or an exit strategy for Afghanistan or Syria. Eradicating Al Qaeda from a place as remote, austere, and hostile as Afghanistan is impossible and roughly equivalent to attempting to end organized crime in the US. I suppose a few tens of thousands of soldiers can achieve in a foreign land what over one million law enforcement professionals in the US have failed to do in the last one hundred years. Why do we continue to fight then? Ask the people getting rich from the wars and you may find your answer.

I propose one additional simple question to Secretary Powell's distinguished list: Is the conflict in the best economic interest of the citizens of the US? No matter what lipstick you would like to put on the pig, war ultimately revolves around money. History does not necessarily serve as a reliable guide in this domain. The world is much more populated and economically interdependent than ever before. There are no new sparsely populated lands to conquer or untapped virgin resources over which to fight. We must, therefore, focus less upon killing people and more on building partnerships and shoring up our economy. After all, domestic prosperity and tranquility are the true strength of the nation, not an armed force capable of defeating the world. The Coronavirus pandemic vividly demonstrates the economic underpinnings of national greatness and further reinforces the logic above. The idea that wars abroad somehow keep us safer at home is yet another Patriotic Illusion with which we must dispense in order to truly be free.

Proposed Reforms

- During time of war, make campaign contributions from Defense Industry illegal.

- Flag-level military Officers forbidden from working for Defense industry upon retirement (lifetime ban).

- Senior Management from Defense Industry forbidden from serving in the Department of Defense (lifetime ban).

- Implement the draft during time of war. The all-volunteer military should only exist in peacetime.

- Congress must reassert its constitutional right to declare war and apply a rigorous framework such as Secretary Powell's questions before initiating hostilities (notwithstanding the President's Emergency War Powers to quickly respond with short-term commitments).

• Forget about the sunk costs of our current wars. Many senior leaders, both in and out of uniform, refuse to let go of our efforts in Iraq, Afghanistan, and Syria. To do so in their minds means that many people died for nothing. Sadly, this is true, but it makes no sense to allow other people to die while we continue to grasp for an exit strategy which does not exist in order to simply save face.

• The President should appoint a Secretary of Defense who loves peace and has an appropriate background running large organizations. Generals and Admirals have a natural predisposition towards conflict—they spend their whole lives preparing for and executing wars. Civilian oversight of the military must provide a counterbalance to these sentiments. Appointing retired senior military personnel to this crucial role simply perpetuates the routine. Admirals and Generals are too often sycophants conditioned by a culture of blind obedience. Notice their unprecedented predominance in the current administration.

• Step down from our moral soap box and begin to negotiate with all Nation's regardless of their track records on human and civil rights. Cultural evolution is a process which takes time. People must see for themselves the intrinsic goodness of championing these equities. Many Nation's do not yet even have control of their food supply and slowly emerge from subsistence economies. Under our current diplomatic engagement strategies, the US would not even have dialogue with our former selves given institutionalized slavery, Native American genocide, and disrespect for women. Yet the greatest potential for positive change lies with the most primitive states.

CHAPTER 4

The Popularity Trap

Popularity should be no scale for the election of
politicians. If it would depend on popularity, Donald
Duck and The Muppets would take seats in senate.

—Orson Welles

I COLLAPSED ONTO THE COUCH in my headquarters completely spent after another long day of military training. Crusty white flakes fell from my fatigues, evidence of a gallon or more of calcified perspiration. All the paratroopers had long since gone home or retired to their rooms in the barracks. As I contemplated the first two months in command of an Airborne Infantry Company, our First Sergeant, the most senior and experienced leader in our organization, burst through the door. He never minced words and I sensed he was about to deliver an ugly message—with the bark on. He gave me a stern look, closed the door behind himself, and said I was failing as a leader because I was too damn friendly, likeable, and accessible. Talk about an attention-grabber! Instead of engaging in a philosophical debate about the relative merits of various leadership styles, I simply asked what I should do about this problem. The First Sergeant replied, "It's simple—*you gotta lay somebody flat* in the next few days or I can't work for you anymore!" Despite my aversion to such an approach, I was too tired to argue, and I needed his support to succeed. The following day, therefore, I found numerous opportunities to chew some butt, and Alpha Company finally got the boss it deserved. The 25 years of leadership experiences since have reinforced the wisdom of the First Sergeant's advice. Allow me to explain.

Subordinates in any organization come in all shapes, sizes, capabilities, and perhaps most important, motivational states. Like every other human trait, motivation, call it the willingness to accomplish your mission or assigned duties, is normally distributed across the population. On the high end, you will have subordinates who are "all in" and will go above and beyond the call of duty; in animal parlance, they are your loyal hounds. On the low end, there will be people who will avoid work at any cost—call them the cats of the world. Getting these folks to do their jobs is like trying to give them a bath; you are likely to get scratched! In the middle of course, you have people who will do what they are told in a timely fashion but will not go looking for extra work. The figure below provides a graphical representation of a generic organization's distribution of motivation.

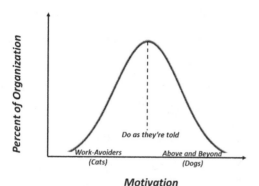

Motivation

Figure 2: Motivation in the Workforce

In my experience, an individual's motivational state is an internal quality which is difficult for others to influence. Many refute this view of the world, however, and claim it is the role of leadership to provide motivation. Even the United States Army, an organization marked by strict discipline and individual accountability, defines leadership as "the process of providing purpose, direction, and ***motivation*** to accomplish the mission and improve the organization".[21] I vehemently reject, however, that it is the leaders' role to "motivate" subordinates. This paradigm shifts responsibility to perform from the subordinate to the leader. The cats of the world will claim they would do their jobs if only they had better leadership; failure is not

21 *Army Field Manual 6-22: Leader Development, June 2015, page 1-3.*
https://armypubs.army.mil/epubs/DR_pubs/DR_a/pdf/web/fm6_22.pdf

their fault. When brought forward for disciplinary action, for instance, they will attempt to turn the tables on the leader by claiming they had insufficient or ambiguous guidance, and this is the root cause of the perceived transgression. It is all just a big misunderstanding boss! A more appropriate definition, therefore, might read it is the role of leadership to provide purpose, direction, and the **proper incentives** to accomplish the mission and improve the organization.

Given the varying motivational states of individuals in an organization as depicted in Figure 2, there is no single effective method for influencing your subordinates. One must adopt a tailored approach and leverage multiple tools to properly incentivize the various creatures in the menagerie. Unfortunately, the dominant dialogue today on the role of leadership in these politically correct times is overly focused upon the power of positivity. Prevailing wisdom reeks of "servant leadership", rainbows, lollipops, and blue ribbons for everyone. Quite nauseating! What about negative reinforcement and fear, are these no longer valid tools? I would bet General George Washington did not carve the Christmas turkey for the motley group of scared and hungry rebels he led across the Delaware one frigid morning to visit unexpected death and destruction upon the Hessian encampment (two colonists died of frostbite on the forced march)[22]. "Boot in ass" was most assuredly an

---

22 Larry Getlen, *The battle that turned a Revolution*, July 4, 2010. https://nypost.com/2010/07/04/the-battle-that-turned-a-revolution/

important and essential ingredient in his leadership cocktail. Have we become so soft as a society that it is no longer acceptable to lead with a firm hand? Consider for a moment the most powerful influencers of human behavior and ask yourself why a leader would not seek to leverage fear under the appropriate circumstances. We humans are biologically hard-wired to vigorously respond to fear. Our very survival depends upon reaction to this primal force and the slackers of the world are unlikely to respond to positive reinforcement.

Leaders also need to wield fear to ensure good order and discipline in their organizations while preventing any dysfunctional or criminal behaviors. Every organization in which I have served in a leadership role, ranging in size from 5 to over 2000, suffered from serious offenses. You may like to think nobody under your charge would behave badly, but if you lead long enough, time will prove you wrong. A leader must assume the best in his subordinates but protect against the worst: trust but verify! Here are some of the behaviors which I addressed in my career which demonstrate my contention:

- Organizational culture where sexual harassment was the norm
- Subordinates running private business endeavors on government time
- Timecard fraud to the tune of tens of thousands of dollars
- Child abuse and neglect
- Supervisors engaging in affairs with their subordinates' spouses

- Illegal substance abuse and trafficking
- Illegal orders to spend millions of dollars of government resources
- Subordinate faking a brain tumor and not showing up to work for two years while privately holding three other jobs.
- Senior leader sexually assaulted his administrative assistant

And many more....

If you inherited these feral creatures, how well do you think you would do "motivating" them to avoid committing the above offenses and crimes? Responsibility clearly lies on the deviant individuals, but a contributing factor in all these cases was a history of a relaxed command climate, in other words, pussyfooted leadership! The only deterrence for these bad actors is fear. All in the organization must understand their leader will bring the full force of the law and other available punishments to deal with such transgressions and will absolutely not accept excuses or transferal of blame. The repercussions of even one such instance mentioned above are broad and deep. The entire organization loses focus on the mission and quickly degrades into a soap opera-like swirl of rumor and gossip, leadership failure by any other name.

So how does a leader stimulate fear in those who need it without running around yelling, bullying, issuing threats, alienating the really great subordinates and earning the title "toxic leader"? Like many arts, it is easier said than done. First and foremost, a leader must uphold organizational standards at all times. The proper foundation is poured on day one with initial counseling which is perhaps the most important act upon assuming a new role. When a leader takes the time to clearly outline expectations, roles and responsibilities, sets a schedule for periodic updates and looks the subordinate in the eyes and says "sign on the dotted line please", the entire organization will know a real boss has finally arrived. One does not even need to discuss specific consequences for falling short of the standards. The very fact that the leader initiated a pointed conversation on the matter provides sufficient evidence for the subordinate to anticipate the hammer if they do not uphold their end of the bargain. The felines of the world will suddenly experience "pucker-factor" as they begin to realize they will be held accountable for everything they do or fail to do. No more will they be allowed to shirk their duties with impunity; a tub of warm water and flea soap is near at hand. But how do the loyal hounds respond to the same conversation: does it invoke trepidation in your over-achievers? Absolutely not, quite the opposite is the case! Those who go above and beyond will now be exhilarated a boss has arrived who will issue "gold stars" and keep a running tally highlighting their individual contributions while also illuminating the shortcomings of the n 'are do wells.

Back to my story. The part about initial counseling I understood well prior to Company Command, and implemented effectively, yet I still managed to lose control of my minions.

What I had failed to anticipate was the power and guile of the cats of the world to avoid the tub. Little by little, I let them get too close to me through informal and seemingly harmless engagements and a generous "open door" policy. Many of these creatures had survived numerous bosses before me and knew a little bootlicking can go a long way to undermine a determined boss. While they have no taste for work, the cats can be tireless butt-kissers. An accommodating boss who places too much faith in the power of positivity can unwittingly provide them the stage on which to perform their feline ju-jitsu. A leader must guard against letting subordinates get too close or comfortable in his presence, a cat can never be your friend! When one nuzzles up to your leg, you must metaphorically kick it across the room for no particular reason other than to show everyone who's in charge. Otherwise, you will soon find yourself surrounded by cats and unable to uphold good order and discipline.

But what of your beloved hounds? Make no mistake, many of them are also sycophants and will seek to lay at your feet and attain favored status. As much as you may dislike doing it, you must also kick them away. If you do not, the felines will take note of the favoritism and report you to the relevant authorities—your Boss, Human Resources, the Union, the Chaplain, the Mayor, the American Civil Liberties Union, Congress, you name it.......anything to avoid the bath! You will then find yourself in a defensive posture trying to justify your actions to multiple entities instead of getting on with your mission and holding folks accountable. Let us not forget your favorite dog is also quite capable of crapping on the rug occasionally. Even the best subordinates sometimes go astray, and the leader must take them out back to the woodshed for disciplinary action. This is far more difficult (and sometimes impossible) to do if you and the dog have become too cozy. He might be man's best friend, but if you are a leader, you are not allowed any such comforts!

If this line of discussion makes you uncomfortable or strikes you as too harsh, do not look for an apology from me. I gave up pussyfooting around decades ago. I would be willing to bet you have a parade of both cats and dogs darkening your door as you read this instead of doing their jobs anyhow so who are you to judge? But it is never too late to decide to do something more than just win the office popularity contest. Do not bullshit yourself, you would probably lose anyhow: people are only nice to you because of your position. Stop searching the internet for motivational quotes; leadership is a contact sport. Get out there into the trenches—kick a butt-sniffing dog, bathe a cat, find somebody to lay flat, and you just might earn your position as head of an organization!

Do not mistake the firm tone I strike above to mean I condone leadership bullying—nothing could be further from the truth. One does not need to act like a jerk to ensure good order and discipline while holding people to high standards of behavior. Unfortunately, I have witnessed time and again toxic subordinates running amok and thriving in all manner of organizations because of a lack of accountability. No one who calls themselves a leader can avoid their responsibility to have tough, uncomfortable conversations with subordinates and check negative behaviors. Failing to do so turns the world upside down and results in unruly subordinates dictating the terms and conditions of their contributions.

Effective leadership does not require popularity. In fact, those who seek it will inevitably fail at both their jobs and earning the affection of their subordinates. Like many other young officers, I initially fell into the trap of leading with my heart instead of my head. It felt good to be liked by those around me even when I occupied positions of command authority. Reflecting on this seemingly innate but counterproductive instinct, I realized that most Americans seek popularity from our earliest school days. We are all directly or indirectly measured by the robustness of our friend network. These forces come to the forefront when we elect class leaders, team captains, prom court, and fall into our respective cliques. All these activities factor into college admission and selection for advanced opportunities in both the public and private sectors. Popular people graduate to leadership roles and quite naturally continue the approval-seeking behaviors which brought them to the dance so to speak. Breaking this cycle is akin to beating a tough addiction which has been reinforced by long-standing habits and the emotional high associated with popularity.

During the course of my two-year long Company Command, the culture of the unit slowly transformed. We began to realize what I call the fruits of the accountability tree. In demanding high standards, our unit earned a positive reputation as standard bearers. Even some of the former cats contributed much more than initially expected. A leader must remember and leverage the fact that most everyone wants to succeed. Like anything else, however, bad behaviors form habits. We become what we repeatedly do. It takes a leader with a firm hand to exert the continuous pressure necessary to help some individuals break their dysfunctional patterns.

In one case, a higher-level Commander directed the assignment of a senior Sergeant First Class to our unit from an adjacent organization. One of my peer Company Commanders claimed this Sergeant was simply rebellious and continuously undermined command guidance. The Sergeant in question had nearly twenty years of experience. This was not a simple matter of adapting to the basics of soldiering and leadership. Something much deeper was in play. Before his first day of work in Alpha Company, we had a long and very frank counselling session, some of which we documented in writing, some not. I made it perfectly clear to the Sergeant that he was under a microscope and I would be watching his every move. I told him my intention was to build a fully documented counselling package to support kicking him out of the Army. Undermining your Commander is serious business and I was not going to put up with any of his bullshit. In his former unit, he was a Platoon Sergeant. I demoted him to one position lower. He would have to serve as a Squad leader. This was a very pointed and serious no-smile zone discussion which occurred in the presence of my First Sergeant. It is important to have a witness during such conversations so nothing can later be misrepresented. Sign on the dotted line please acknowledging that you understand your role and what is expected of you. When that bit of ugliness was over, I folded up the counselling file and placed it in a locked drawer in my desk. I then assumed a more relaxed tone and talked to the Sergeant man to man as equals. I let him know that I respected his knowledge and experience and had every intention of leveraging his significant abilities. Whatever bad blood existed between him and his previous Commander did not matter, he had a clean slate with me. My goal for him was to reinstate him as a Platoon Sergeant within three months if he could prove that he deserved the position. And that counseling file we had just created, it could cut both ways to either help or hurt him. We were going to meet at the end of every week to talk about and document his progress. We could either fill it up with glowing accolades and compliments—evidence to support reinstatement, or it could be a bag of dogshit which I would use to throw him out of the Army. The ball was in his court.

What happened next still causes tears to well up despite the over twenty years since this drama unfolded. This Sergeant transformed into the best damn Non-Commissioned Officer in the entire Battalion. For context, we had approximately fifty such leaders at his level in our ranks. He quickly regained his status as a Platoon Sergeant and was my most energetic and loyal subordinate. Loyalty is a two-way rifle range. In order to receive it, you must also give it away. His performance was so far above any of his peers that I advocated for him to leave my Company and work at a higher level as the Battalion Master Trainer. Teaching and inspiring young paratroopers was his special gift. The Battalion Commander who formerly wanted me to run this Sergeant out of the Army now embraced him as his best and brightest trainer. The transformation resulted directly from accountability. When it was time for me to move on, this Sergeant came and found me to personally say farewell. He said that first conversation in my office was forever burned into his memory and he never wanted to have another one like it in his life. We remained in touch for many years after we went our separate ways and I remember him very fondly. I benefited as much or more from our mutual relationship. He validated in my mind the value of rejecting popularity-seeking behaviors in favor of direct and brutally honest conversations.

Regarding discipline, two personal vignettes briefly mentioned in the above bulleted list merit further exploration. The first instance involved a Colonel who allegedly sexually assaulted his administrative assistant after excessive consumption of alcoholic beverages while on duty. The administrative assistant kept the incident secret for several months until she finally broke down and notified authorities. The military conducted an initial investigation and found enough substantiating evidence to remove the Colonel from his command position. I temporarily replaced this officer and thus had a front-row seat to the unfolding drama. When the formal investigation concluded after approximately four months, higher headquarters offered the alleged rapist a choice between administrative punishment with no recourse or face criminal charges in a formal court martial. Of course, the Colonel chose administrative action which amounted to losing a month's pay (approximately $10,000) and retirement with an "other than honorable" discharge from the military. Who in their right mind would risk a trial by peers and end up in jail for a very long time when they could instead skate away with a mere slap on the hand? The Colonel moved on with his life and retired with a full pension and benefits. The retired Colonel quickly found another job and moved on with his life. The victim, however, suffered a very different fate. Her husband divorced her because he concluded his wife must have been complicit in the alleged sexual encounter if the officer was not seriously punished. She also attempted suicide because her life was ruined. Would you be happy with this "justice" if your daughter had potentially been raped? Why was the officer not held accountable for such a serious offense which should have seen him check into the cross-bar hotel for many years? As it turns out, a senior officer at higher headquarters in a position to decide whether or not to pursue criminal charges had a pre-existing personal relationship with the Colonel defendant. Additionally, the broader military community struggled with a tidal wave of sexual assault in the ranks during this timeframe. Many Congressman even felt the authority to prosecute such offenses needed to transfer from military to civilian authorities. Nobody in the uniformed power positions, therefore, had incentive to bring this embarrassing case into the light of day.... unless of course they had a moral compass and actually cared about doing the right thing more than covering their butts.

In the second case, I kicked over a hornet's nest when I discovered an Army Major had faked a serious illness at an outpost far removed from my headquarters. Upon first visiting this outpost in my new role, the Navy officer in charge, one of my subordinates, greeted me with the typical "dog and pony" show designed to highlight the technical contributions of his unit. The Army Major who worked for the Navy officer was not present, so I inquired about his status.

Navy officer—"Sir, Major X is really sick. He has a brain tumor and is undergoing chemotherapy."

My reply—"Let's go see him right now then, what hospital is he at?"

The Navy officer who had over twenty years of leadership experience had no clue regarding the Major's whereabouts. I found this highly curious. Given my time constraints and subsequent travel plans, however, I allowed the dog and pony show to continue. Upon returning to my headquarters, I directed the Navy officer to send me the medical documentation regarding the Major's status. He initially hid behind unfounded health privacy concerns but soon produced laughably inadequate documentation which did not indicate the Major had a serious condition. As fate would have it, the Major's retirement paperwork landed on my desk for approval at the same time. Buried deep within the packet, I noticed Major X had waived his right to a retirement physical intended to document his medical condition for any potential disabilities. This is highly unusual for any officer to waive, especially one with a brain tumor. Something very rotten was afoot and I went into bloodhound mode launching a formal investigation into the Major's true status. The investigator quickly found Major X had not reported for military duty for over a year while still drawing full pay and allowances as an active duty officer. Additionally, he worked as a bar tender and real estate manager on the side and had no serious medical issues. These shocking results quickly reached the three-star level of awareness and the shit hit the fan. The General who I worked for was embarrassed because he had been in charge for over two years and given Major X positive evaluation reports without ever really getting to know him. Much like the Navy officer, he simply accepted the Major's word regarding his status and did not verify. The General expressed frustration with me for launching the investigation because the whole event made him look bad. In other words, my actions damaged the impression the three-star had of him and would thus hurt his outlook for further promotion. This was the final nail in my professional coffin, and I retired shortly thereafter. I made the mistake of actually caring about a subordinate's condition enough to dig into the details without thinking through the political ramifications. Holding other's accountable is not what gets you ahead. It is also not what makes you popular with either seniors or subordinates. There is something desperately wrong with this state of affairs, but the military is by no means unique in this domain.

Consider for a moment the police officer who murdered George Floyd in Minneapolis touching off a national upheaval against police brutality. Derek Chauvin, the accused murderer, allegedly had 18 complaints filed with the police department's internal affairs division only two of which were closed with discipline. Call me crazy, but this many potential offenses sounds like a pattern. Who was Mr. Chauvin's immediate supervisor and what did this person do about his behavior? Why were appropriate standards for arrest and detention not enforced? Three other officers on the scene did not feel compelled to correct the situation even in the face of a man pleading for his life. This was no accident, it resulted from a pattern of behavior and a deep-rooted dysfunctional culture. Countless leaders had advanced through the ranks of the Minneapolis Police department for years, probably decades, while remaining complicit with this environment. Derek Chauvin is not the only individual with blood on his hands. This monumental tragedy resulted from pussyfooted, popularity-seeking leadership. Easier to just go along to get along than to make people uncomfortable by calling for reform and taking punitive action. Making waves is not how you get ahead in any organization in the United States. People occupying positions of power and influence all across America avoid holding others accountable. It is a dying art.

Real leaders, however, should make people uncomfortable. They ask tough questions, demand excellence from subordinates, and challenge both conventional wisdom and authority when necessary. New stressors provide the impetus for personal and professional growth and there is no one more effective at injecting tension into the workforce than the head of the organization. This does not mean leaders should rule with an iron fist and alienate subordinates. Making people squirm in the appropriate fashion is a delicate artform which requires balance.

I. *Asking tough questions*

Consider the example of a formal and detailed program status update to the boss. Subordinates will collect all manner of financial, schedule and technical metrics for discussion. Whether the team has good news, bad news, or a mixed bag, every presenter should bring their "A" game and approach the forum with trepidation. After all, their leader has walked a mile in their shoes and performed superbly or he would not have earned his position. The boss must possess considerable insight into the data presented and see deeply enough to challenge friction points or logical disconnects which the team perhaps missed. The best way to help subordinates see these is to ask non-threatening questions which illuminate the issues of concern. A leader, however, must never insult anyone's intelligence, professionalism, or dedication, especially in public, as this will immediately provoke resentment and mistrust. Toxic individuals lay blame, threats, and accusations while inspired leaders build mutual trust, common understanding and dedication. The key to success lies in asking more and telling less.

In such organizational meetings, saying nothing of value is almost as bad as acting inappropriately. If a leader fails to contribute to the discussion, he lacks the mastery necessary to wield influence. Some remain silent in accordance with the old adage "Better to be thought a fool than to open your mouth and remove all doubt". In this unfortunate case, his technical ineptitude quickly conditions to team to relax—nothing to worry about here. The boss will simply revert to platitudes, high fives, and pats on the back. He leads in name only and therefore seeks popularity as a substitute for useful content. Unfortunately, feeling good is not the same as actually being good. Diamonds only form from sustained pressure.

II. *Demanding the best from subordinates*

Leaders must also drive their subordinates' professional development and demand positive progress. The first and most important act upon taking charge should be to counsel direct reports. In this forum, one sets the tone for all future interactions—the importance of the engagement cannot be overstated. The best questions a leader can ask a subordinate early in their relationship is "where do you want to go, what are you doing to get there, and how can I help?" These require the subordinate to set goals and accept the career challenges necessary to grow. It lays the groundwork for demanding excellence from subordinates while also acknowledging the leader's responsibility to provide the three T's: the Time, Training, and Tools necessary to succeed. Doing the same old thing year in and year out only makes you better at your current job; it does not prepare you for an exceptional future. The leader will likely receive many "deer in the headlights" reactions to this line of inquiry. The appropriate response in this event is to challenge the subordinate to return to the next meeting with answers. It is okay to give them time to think about these crucial issues, but by no means should one let them off the hook. If the subordinate returns to the next scheduled formal counseling session with no answers, immediately throw them out of the office with guidance to return when they are ready to have a pointed discussion on the topic. Yes, this will make them uncomfortable. A leader should take this as a positive sign he is doing his job. Heading up an organization does not demand popularity, but it does require setting and enforcing high standards and proactively providing the resources subordinates need to succeed.

III. *Challenge conventional wisdom and authority*

Independent thought lies at the heart of strong leadership. No matter how many individuals contribute to framing a problem and proposing potential solutions, the leader alone must choose the course. In this sense, he is very much alone and must therefore be comfortable thinking for himself. While most bosses value "Get 'r done" subordinates, blind obedience is a goose-stepping formula for disaster. Those who never challenge authority or conventional wisdom have become intellectually lazy and therefore lack the ability to act appropriately in the absence of guidance from higher authority. Additionally, consider the unfortunate instance when an illegal, immoral, or unnecessarily dangerous turd rolls down the hill and into one's lap. What then—just do it without challenge or debate? Knowing what to do when conventional wisdom fails or when to push back against your boss requires strong leaders. Unfortunately, these qualities also make people uncomfortable—especially higher authority who feels the pressure to accomplish objectives and holds the keys to his subordinates' advancement.

Everyone loves to work for a person who makes them feel good about themselves and their respective contributions to the group. High-fives in the board room and big holiday bonuses for all leave the entire team in a state of euphoria. Unfortunately, these emotional highs do little to advance either individual or group objectives. Good feelings also quickly disintegrate in the face of organizational adversity. A team must then rely on collective competencies to fight its way out of the corner. Encountering hardships for the first time when an emergency lands at the doorstep is a recipe for failure. Contrary to populist sentiment, therefore, leaders must strive to make people uncomfortable. Personal and organizational excellence are born in the shadow of discomfort: accountability, tough questions, high expectations, and the tension of respectful disagreement. Being good is far more important than the short-lived high of feeling good.

Proposed Reforms

America's leadership crisis is largely due to the lack of accountability. While everyone wants a quick win such as a passage of new legislation or policy to prevent such tragedies, they will not yield the desired results because we have the wrong leaders in charge at all levels. These individuals exercise great power and discretion to subvert the will of the people. When given a choice between the harder right and the easier wrong, a weak or immoral leader will fail every time. The US got into this situation little by little through a stacking of tolerances and we must back out of it in the same fashion. Implementing measures to help ensure the rise of the right people in leadership roles who will promote a culture of fairness, high moral principles and justice for all is the first step. Leader advancement in any career domain must be informed by tangible evidence an individual spends their time on adding value to the organization and its people and not just tending to personal image and exposure.

- Physically produce counseling files for all direct-report subordinates which demonstrate setting high standards which are frequently revisited to gauge progress. For the most part, people do best what the boss checks. If you do not check, you effectively tell your subordinates it is not important. Over the course of a thirty-year military career, I never received effective and sustained counseling from a boss. In most cases, I also drafted the words for my performance appraisals. This was not as beneficial to me as it may appear on the surface because the words are mostly irrelevant in the Army's evaluation system. Delegating this to the rated officer simply saves the boss from having to take time to think and write about his subordinates' contributions and potential. An officer's boss's boss reserves the box check which quantifies your performance against your peers. This alone determines whether or not you will advance.

- Quantify the disciplinary infractions which occurred on the leader's team during a reporting period and how they were handled. Fully assessing these takes focus and time, but provides insights into the leader's judgement, sense of justice and balance: essential traits for positions of significant responsibility.

- Quantify the trend of team infractions during the leader's tenure. A downward trend usually indicates a leader who enforces high standards and holds people accountable. An upward trend points towards pussyfooted leadership.

• Review the results of a 360-degree survey of the leader's performance. Such results provide valuable insights into what subordinates, peers, and other seniors think about a rising leader. Do not confuse this as a popularity competition. Depending on the content, negative survey results from subordinates may indicate effective leadership. For instance, a subordinate might whine about a boss who insists on maintaining high standards. My First Sergeant loved to say "If the soldiers aint complaining, we must not be training." The people grading and assessing the rising leader must take the time to carefully read and analyze these inputs which create a word picture of the complete individual which is much more complete than a simple box check.

• Quantify results which show leader engagement in the personal and professional growth of subordinates:

  – How many people on the team were promoted?

  – How many people took advantage of educational and advanced training opportunities?

  – How did subordinate performance improve in measurable ways?

– Organizational turbulence—high retention usually indicates subordinates are thriving while low retention might mean people are fleeing poor leadership.

CHAPTER 5

Anyone can be a Leader

Innovation distinguishes between a leader and a follower.
—Steve Jobs

I HAVE GROWN TO DESPISE the "everyone is a leader" mantra. If this holds true, the distinction between leaders and followers has no meaning. Furthermore, life has taught me most people usually simply follow and possess the qualities of sheep—happy to go with the flow and unwilling to make waves. If you have ever served in a large organization, for instance, you have probably noticed nothing ever really changes and the people at the top of the food chain capable of making things better are either unable or unwilling to act. This is because they are sheep sitting upon a throne more aptly suited for a lion—a strong independent person capable of creative thought and decisive action.

Sheep are creatures of habit who rarely ever generate an original idea and simply live out their days grazing upon whatever pasture in which they find themselves. They attain positions of authority through various means such as hard work, loyalty to superiors, political skill, technical expertise, popularity, and sometimes good old-fashioned nepotism, but none of these equate to leadership. Leaders stand apart as do lions on the savannah. They could never be confused as mere members of the flock. Most of us recognize a great leader when we encounter one, yet we struggle with defining the essence of what makes them special other than the fact that we admire them and would willing do their bidding.

Leaders are born much more so than they are trained or nurtured. Deep down, you know the truth of this even if you dislike the implication that despite the best training and experiences available, it is impossible to convert a sheep into a lion. Leading requires the exertion of more energy than following and entails taking risks which members of the flock do not share. In other words, possessing the attributes of a leader is a genetic gamble: high risk, uncertain reward. In settings which lack significant environmental stressors, leaders fade into the background as maintaining the status quo provides the ideal conditions for all to thrive. This is why lions are a rare and special breed in the modern world; we have become complacent in prosperity. There are no new lands to explore or significant threats to human survival; we inherited a sheepish world.

Nevertheless, true leaders serve as a crucial insurance policy for humanity—break glass in case of an emergency. Who would know Winston Churchill, for instance, if not for the crisis that World War II imposed upon Great Britain and the Allied Powers? He recognized the emerging threat of Nazi Germany long before his contemporaries and knew that England's policy of appeasement would end catastrophically. Mr. Churchill was a *change agent*, and this is the essence of true leadership. Maintaining the routine in prosperous times simply requires excellent administrators and managers, bureaucrats by any other name. Influencing the herd to move against its will into unknown territory, however, requires a unique set of skills. Change agent attributes include 1) the ability to anticipate the need to adapt, 2) creativity to generate viable alternatives, 3) a willingness to take the risks associated with championing change, and 4) strong intra-personal and organizational skills to see the task through to the end.

Sheep do not question the establishment or what makes the clock tick even though they can be incredibly intelligent and highly educated. One will gaze up at the blue sky and think "what a lovely day to graze in the pasture", head back down to the ground. A leader, however, has thought deeply about the sky, why it is blue, and what it can tell us about the future. The leader will notice the types of clouds and how fast they are moving and might decide it is time to prod the herd down the mountain into the tree-line to seek shelter from a coming storm. In other words, he anticipates the need to change course long before the masses realize the peril. The trademark qualities which enable this are the powers of keen observation and inquisitiveness. Leaders are more mentally active and see the world at a deeper level than followers. This trait manifests at a very young age. Every parent or elementary school teacher can attest to the exhausting string of questions an intensely curious child can launch.

Unfortunately, the sheep who run our daily lives quickly grow impatient with repeated inquiries and create an environment which disincentivizes the spirit of curiosity. After all, there is a set program of instruction to complete and there is no time to intellectually stray from the beaten path—bah. A blossoming leader might wonder why humans have a base 10 number system as opposed to binary (base 2) or the more efficient hexadecimal (base 6), and instead of completing his multiplication facts worksheet (8 x 7 = 56, 8 x 8 = 64, blah, blah, blah), he may pause and pose this question to the class. This will probably make the teacher who is almost certainly a sheep intensely uncomfortable as such things have never occurred to him even though the answer is in plain sight—humans usually have 10 digits on our hands (numerous cultural hearths with no communication independently developed a base 10 number system). From early childhood, individuals who might blossom into leaders, therefore, face an uphill fight. They stand apart from the herd yet face overwhelming pressure to conform instead of exploring new ground and alternative paths. But how can a person who develops the habit of simply fitting in and going along ever hope to set a course into unchartered territory and convince others to follow?

Upon recognizing the need to change, a leader must then consider the range of options available and conduct a cost-benefit analysis of sorts. The best leaders craft "out of the box" solutions; courses of action that are unorthodox and radically different than any previously attempted tried and true methods. The lion does not have to go it alone during this phase. It is wise to pose the challenge to other members of the team and trusted subordinates to seek their inputs; even the ovine minions will likely offer something of value. Many minds are better than one when it comes to creative problem solving, but some issues are true dilemmas to which there is no clearly superior approach. No matter how many individuals contribute to framing the issue and generating options, the leader alone must decide on the best approach, and in this sense, he is very much alone. The toughest problems are those for which there is little or no historical or organizational context. This presents the lion with a blank canvas and generating a framework for decision making is thus largely a creative process. How many individuals do you know who occupy leadership positions today are truly creative and do you believe this is a trait which can be learned? In my experience, artistic talents appear to be intrinsic much more so than they are learned, and very few people in positions of authority have ever created anything new or unique. Many gain unmerited positive reputations thanks to the keen ability to find flaws in the work of others. Such a leader might point out inconsistent fonts, formats, or color schemes but offer precious little of real substance. Far easier to critique than to do or to create—we must recognize this crucial distinction.

Many leaders today attain their status without taking personal or professional risks. Thirty years in the United States Army vividly demonstrated for me even one risky decision gone awry or one professional disagreement with a superior can end an aspiring leader's career. I have first-hand experience in this domain and have witnessed the end of many emerging leaders at the hands of incompetent, insecure, or corrupt senior commissioned officers. In one such instance, an Army General repeatedly attempted to coerce a subordinate into breaking both the law and Department of Defense regulations as they pertain to the development of advanced weapon systems. Even worse than breaking the law yourself is using the power of your position to browbeat others into violations on your behalf. To the subordinate's credit, he resisted the pressure and refused to compromise his integrity. Unfortunately, his career ended prematurely thanks to a single negative evaluation from the General.

Independent thought, moral character, and risk taking are not what gets you ahead in large organizations. Compliance and unconditional loyalty to superiors serve as the coin of the wooly realm. This is the primary reason why change agents do not typically occupy positions of significant power today. Nevertheless, the willingness to take risks is an essential element of true leadership. President Lincoln provides an excellent example of a crucial lion in American history. He took the risks associated with preserving the Union and led the Nation through a cataclysmic civil war which few politicians of the day had the courage to support. He also assumed the risk of ending the abhorrent practice of slavery in conjunction with reconciling longstanding cultural differences between the North and South. In short, he resolved the issues which the revered founders left lingering due to their inability to reach a morally and legally acceptable solution at the birth of our Nation. Tragically, taking these risks and leading the United States into the future resulted in Lincoln's assassination, but where would we be today without his leadership?

Leaders—change agents, must not shrink from the unknown. It is their crucial responsibility to accept the risks associated with embarking on a new endeavor of unpredictable outcome. Otherwise, well trained sheep can simply maintain the current routine. Risk taking is not an easily learned trait. Some individuals simply have a higher tolerance than others. Everyone can recall childhood peers and identify a few who displayed more of a willingness to break the mold. They are the types who are early-adopters of skateboarding, tackle football, surfing, bicycle motocross, gymnastics, skydiving, martial arts, etc.: activities in which an individual is more likely to suffer personal injury than more traditional hobbies. The allure associated with risk taking is in our DNA; a sheep will never comprehend the "stupid" chances a lion is willing to take. Try as they might, the sheep of the world will simply never voluntarily stray from the herd.

In a recent debate with an Army colleague, we both lamented the behavior of a particular three star general because he refused to make a low-risk decision potentially producing remarkable benefits for the entire service. Further exacerbating the matter, said three star had climbed to the very top of his profession and had no potential to ever be a four star. Taking the risk had no career downside for him. The most plausible explanation is that he was, is, and always will be a sheep. We must not confuse one's organizational position with the ability to lead. He clearly incrementally climbed to the top of the military pyramid through hard work, political savvy, and avoiding risk at every turn, but he can no more shed his wooly cloak than a lion can become a vegetarian.

Physical and moral courage both correlate to the willingness to accept risk. An individual who voluntarily participates in dangerous activities puts his personal well-being on the line. A person who refuses to comply with an illegal or immoral directive issued from his boss or other powerful authority puts the fate of his career at stake. These are necessary qualities for a lion as bravery is required to withstand the pressure exerted by the establishment when it attempts to snuff his initiative, end his career, reject his vision, or demand that he get back in line with the flock. The best leaders whom I have encountered were fearless in the face of conflict and completely frank with subordinates and seniors alike when expressing the perils associated with inappropriate or dangerous guidance. Unfortunately for team lion, these individuals are unlikely to climb to the top of the pyramid as they will encounter a never-ending series of sheep, some of whom will envy the leadership qualities they see in a young cub which are lacking in themselves. Having a boss who is professionally or personally jealous rarely ends well for the subordinate.

The most cunning of sheepish authorities, however, will sometimes keep a caged lion as a pet. The devious wooly bastard will pretend to mentor the lion and occasionally toss him red meat as a reward for harvesting his good ideas while passing them off as his own. Make no mistake though, the ovine council will never allow the lion to roam free as this would be far too dangerous to the established order. A host of sheep is highly unlikely to ever let a lion to advance through their ranks to a position of significant influence. This will only occur when external conditions create a perfect storm and a crisis arises to which the herd has no answer.

Once the leader sets his organization moving in a new direction, the battle to keep the herd on course is just beginning. Unforeseen troubles and setbacks are sure to arise, and the followers will likely see every hardship as supporting evidence to revert to their former pastures; turn back before it is too late! The lion must endure the incessant bleating of the mob and provide constant reassurance. The skills required to keep everyone on track and marching towards the leaders' vision are those more traditionally viewed as leadership: task organization, oral and written communication, intra-personal skills, emotional intelligence, personal presence, counselling, etc. This is a realm where experience, call it saddle time, pays dividends as such skills can be honed with practice if the leader possesses a sustained commitment to self-improvement. Sheep can also be quite capable in this domain, and this is how they often masquerade as leaders. Of particular importance during this phase, the lion must provide the sheep with periodic updates that demonstrate positive progress or alternatively, explain the plan to overcome unexpected obstacles. In the absence of confidence and close physical proximity to their leader, the sheep may simply stop or worse yet, attempt to reverse direction returning to more familiar ground. Once the goal is obtained, however, the most capable in the flock will likely claim credit for supporting and achieving the new end-state. They will seek to slowly marginalize the lion as his particular skill set is no longer needed in much the same fashion as Winston Churchill was quickly relegated to a political persona non grata after World War II. Nobody wanted to heed his roaring about the need to address the threat posed by Soviet Russia; the herd was ready to settle down into a new pasture. This is the way of the world. Even the mightiest lion cannot overcome a mob of back-stabbing, ankle-biting sheep.

The term leadership is used so loosely today that it has become almost meaningless. We use the same moniker for great athletes, bureaucrats, and military commanders, for instance, when very few of these admittedly talented individuals ever had an original idea or voluntarily stuck their necks out to take a chance on a risky undertaking. In short, they are not change agents; they are merely well-accomplished sheep. The first lemming in the pack headed towards cliff's edge and certain death, for instance, is simply the fastest runner in a mindless pack, but by modern standards, we would applaud its physical prowess and label it a leader. When real change agents emerge to solve a crisis and lead us in a new direction, all recognize and celebrate their unique talents. As soon as the emergency is over, however, and society reaches a new and acceptable equilibrium, the lions of the world are rejected; long-term coexistence is impossible.

Leaders are a rare breed, and despite the bumper stickers, you probably will not find that they attain high office in politics, the military, professional sports, or academic institutions. Climbing to the top in these professions requires popularity, extraordinary personal commitment, sacrifice, athletic and intellectual excellence respectively. These roles do not require creative problem solvers willing to take risks and influence others to follow them into the unknown. In fact, there are considerable disincentives to behave in such a fashion. These organizations may as well hang a sign that reads "Leaders need not apply" as the lion's unique talents are largely unneeded today given our collective prosperity. Nevertheless, lions are born into every generation and hail from all walks of life. You are likely to find them running their own small businesses, cutting new ground as entrepreneurs, working in high-risk occupations and other solo endeavors where they do not have to answer to "the man". Lions do not willingly or easily submit to the authority of sheep. They also undoubtedly exist in our inner cities where individuals reject the status quo, and therefore learn to think for themselves; the first and most important leadership prerequisite.

Despite the fact that change agents do not currently occupy significant leadership positions, the age of the lion draws nigh. Storm clouds are forming on the horizon. Persistent social issues, unsustainable government spending, the reemergence of a multi-polar international community, and an over-committed military all indicate the coming need for radical change—a shift out of our comfort zone into new and unexplored territory. Who will you follow when the world comes unhinged and our current "leaders" drive the bus off the cliff due to their inability to change direction? If you put your head down and stay behind the sheep who got us into this mess in the first place, you will most assuredly land on the wrong side of history not so different from individuals who opposed Abraham Lincoln when he served as a crucial change agent to alter the direction of American society. Your faith will be much better placed in a lion who offers a compelling and radically different vision while the sheep of the world stand paralyzed and incapable of positive action. You had best learn to recognize the requisite traits now or a pretender will likely pull the wool over your eyes. If we wish to elevate lions to more prominent roles in public service, we must start by reimagining the education of our children from square one.

Proposed Reforms

- Include change agent attributes (independent reasoning, creativity, risk taking, and intra-personal skills) as leadership selection criteria in both the private and public domains.

- Work to eradicate the influences of nepotism, wealth, and political connections.

- Downplay the importance of academic achievement when selecting people for advanced leadership opportunities.

CHAPTER 6

The Communists are Coming

Communism has never come to a country that was
not disrupted by war or corruption or both.
—John F. Kennedy

DOING IS THE ENEMY of thinking. If you can slow down for a minute, let that idea sink in! The rat race of our daily lives prevents most people from contemplating important issues because of the pressure to accomplish a never-ending host of tasks. The mere absence of activity makes us nervous. Better to do something than nothing so we sometimes busy ourselves rearranging the chairs on the deck of the Titanic so to speak. We even select our leaders based mostly upon how long they are willing to work instead of the results they produce. The fruits of a leader's labors may not manifest for years, but punching the clock is immediately obvious and measurable. No loafers allowed on the bus. As a person prone to thinking before acting, however, I detest the dedication litmus test. Us "lazy" folk often find the easiest and most efficient ways of doing things. Intellectual sloth is just as real and certainly more crippling than its physical counterpart.

As an example, consider how Americans are responding to the Coronavirus crisis. Toilet paper is one of the hottest commodities. This pathetic exhibition supports the doing versus thinking thesis. As the world grinds to a halt, of all things to worry about, Americans urgently address wiping their butts as though no viable household options exist. One need only take a moment to come up with a dozen alternatives to the venerable TP—napkins, paper towels, that drawer full of unmatched socks, old t-shirts, a washcloth, or perish the thought, a shower to cleanse your derriere. Coronavirus reveals our very ugly state of intellectual decay. America has an abundance of accomplished doers of deeds yet is woefully short on thinkers. And now that all the busy bodies find themselves confined to their homes, whatever shall they do? Clean the grill, wash the baseboards, unpack long forgotten boxes in the attic? Anything to stay engaged and avoid being alone with their thoughts.

As the world slows down and we all have far less to do, we should spend this idle time thinking. Consider for a moment how the global economy has responded to the pandemic. Supply chains all over the world ground to a halt. Factory closures in China and Europe created knock-on effects here in the United States and vice-versa. The international marketplace is far more connected and interdependent than ever before presenting a new strategic framework. During the Cold War, Mutually Assured Destruction (MAD) kept the peace and prevented full spectrum conflict between nuclear armed powers. The modern condition of deeply intertwined trade further reinforces this strategic stalemate through Irreversibly Ruined Economies or IRE for short. How could we possibly go to war with China and Russia when doing so would halt all means of global production? No electricity, no food, no fresh water, no medicine, no war....and that is a good thing! Even if we could stockpile enough weapons and supplies for our military to fight a protracted conflict with a peer foe, our people would immediately be denied life's necessities. What would be the point of such a war if society completely collapses?

I hope our leaders stop to think about IRE and appropriately modify our diplomatic and military engagement strategies. I also hope they take time to think about protecting our people from a host of other threats aside from terrorism and the Coronavirus to include opioid addiction (approximately 75,000 American deaths per year), murders (approximately 16,000 per year) and suicides (approximately 50,000 per year). If you take a moment to think about it, domestic prosperity, not a military capable of conquering the world is the true strength of our nation.

Our first responsibility as citizens and leaders is to think before acting; an apparently forgotten art. The present crisis should force us to slow down and reevaluate our priorities. Our national leadership, however, continues to insist we must prepare for a war with the communists—namely China and Russia. Here is an excerpt from the 2018 National Defense Strategy:

> *Inter-state strategic competition, not terrorism, is now the primary concern in U.S. national security. China is a strategic competitor using predatory economics to intimidate its neighbors while militarizing features in the South China Sea. Russia has violated the borders of nearby nations and pursues veto power over the economic, diplomatic, and security decisions of its neighbors.*[23]

As the American public slowly grows weary of the Global Wars on Terror, the hawks and fear-mongers must find and prop up new threats to justify bloated defense budgets. Enter two easy to hate perennial foes, China, and Russia. Given their communist political systems, Americans immediately see red without much further thought. Our deep-rooted fear of this political and economic framework dates all the way back to the Bolshevik revolution led by Vladimir Lenin in 1917. Let us take a moment to really think about the dangers these

---

23 Jim Mattis, *Summary of the 2018 National Defense Strategy*, US Department of Defense

nations pose to the United States. Will they invade Hawaii and subsequently launch an amphibious invasion of California? If you believe this, please explain how such a conventional conflict fails to escalate into nuclear warfare when one party begins to lose. The strategic MAD stalemate still applies. Additionally, what about IRE? How do any participants maintain the logistical support to supply combat formations when global supply chains shut down? Have any grown-ups really stopped to think about these issues?

Short of an actual fighting war, China poses other very serious threats. The US Federal Bureau of Investigation has opened approximately 1000 cases involving corporate theft and espionage by the Chinese and estimates it steals roughly $300 to $600 Billion per year from the US.[24] The Chinese, for instance, recently fielded an advanced jet aircraft, the J-31 which looks to be an exact replica of the US F-35 Lightning—our most advanced fighter jet. The F-35 cost the US taxpayer tens of billions of dollars to develop and the Chinese avoided these costs by simply copying our design. Building more and more weapons for a shooting war that will never happen, therefore, does not make sense. It also will not prevent our enemies from simply copying those designs as well as finding ways to exploit their vulnerabilities. The real threat

---

24 The Guardian, *China Theft of Technology is Biggest Law Enforcement Threat to US says FBI*, February 6, 2020. https://www.theguardian.com/world/2020/feb/06/china-technology-theft-fbi-biggest-threat

is intellectual theft and the US is doing almost nothing to stop this. We must move to keep trade secrets and weapon designs off the internet and away from unvetted personnel who come to the US to spy under the auspices of studying at some of our finest institutions. Pouring ever more resources into defense without turning off these gates is akin to trying to fill a bottomless bucket.

Yet the ill-advised and misplaced saber rattling continues by US strategic thinkers of all varieties. When you openly and repeatedly call someone your enemy, they behave accordingly. The US deploys carrier groups and conducts aerial combat patrols all along the coast of China and then has the audacity to label Chinese counter actions provocative. If the Chinese ran such patrols off the West Coast of the United States, would we not deploy ships to meet them and develop new weapons and tactics to destroy them in the event of a shooting war? Of course we would. Who is really the provocateur? Consider the relative military budgets in Figure 3 on the following page.[25] Based solely on military expenditures, does it look the United States risks being overrun by communist China and Russia? We should therefore not allow those who profit from perpetuating the global arms race to stoke the American public into spending

---

25 Stockholm International Peace Research Institute, *Global Military Budgets See Largest Annual Increase in a Decade*, https://www.sipri.org/media/press-release/2020/global-military-expenditure-sees-largest-annual-increase-decade-says-sipri-reaching-1917-billion, 27 April 2020.

ever more on defense. The United States spends more on defense then the next ten biggest spenders combined. Maybe we should rename the Department of Defense the Department of Offense.

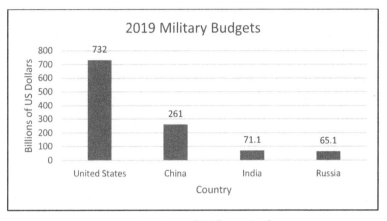

Figure 3: National Military Budgets

Setting aside toe-to-toe conflict with the communist foes, American strategists contend we must protect Taiwan and the Ukraine from China and Russia, respectively. Why? Do you believe young Americans should fight and die to prop up the regimes of these two countries? The Ukraine only recently achieved independence from Russia when the former Soviet Union collapsed in economic disarray in 1991. Ukrainian Nationalist leaders took advantage of the situation and seized control of the vast economic and agricultural resources of their region which historically served as Russia's breadbasket. Since reconstituting, however, Mother Russia has decided it wants its groceries back. Who are we to stop them? American politicians cut deals with foreign politicians but want we the people of the United States to believe we are somehow championing the freedom of those poor, downtrodden Ukrainians and must underwrite their promises and business deals with our lives. If the Russians regain control, however, the day to day happenings of the people there will likely remain largely unchanged. The only losers, therefore, are the Ukrainian politicians wielding power and controlling the flow of money and resources some of which lands in the pockets of American politicians. Hunter Biden for instance, the son of former Vice President Joe Biden, served as a ceremonial figure for one of the Ukraine's largest energy companies—Burisma Holdings from 2014 to 2019. During this timeframe, Hunter Biden received $83,333 per month for "consulting services".[26] Ask yourself if Hunter Biden knows anything about the Ukrainian energy business and how he could possibly be worth a million dollars per year to them? It does not pass the commonsense check. Our policy of defending Ukrainian "freedom", therefore, is not so much altruistic as it is a dart in Russia's ass and a check in the pockets of a few American leaders. We seek to deny Russia their former sovereign territory to limit their national power and clout. In doing so, however, we shape Russia's confrontational stance and perpetuate the enmity between our nations. If this lukewarm war ever goes hot, it will not be the sons and daughters of American and Ukrainian power players who fight

---

26 Brie Stimson, *Hunter Biden got $83G per month for "ceremonial"* gig: report, Fox News, October 18, 2019.

and die. Our leaders will instead recruit, train, and arm the masses to do their bidding while filling them with patriotic fervor. Our political and military leaders will undoubtedly peddle the idea we must stop the Red horde as far forward as possible or they will soon knock on our doors too! Have you not seen the popular American movie *Red Dawn*?

What if the shoe were on the other foot, and California suddenly broke away from the US in the turmoil caused by COVID19 and civil strife in the Summer of 2020? The US would most assuredly work to bring California back into the fold by any means possible. Would we tolerate Russian interference with this objective?

Similar logic applies to Taiwan. Chinese Nationalists fled to Taiwan in 1949 and established a new Capitol after forfeiting control of mainland China to Communist forces. The people of Taiwan are Chinese and most have relatives on the mainland. How much will their lives really change if reunited under the Communist regime of mainland China? Probably not at all. The only losers will be Nationalist politicians who will have to step down and flee for their lives and US defense industry which profits from robust foreign military sales. Taiwan has purchased tens of billions of dollars in US defense equipment to include fighter jets, heavy tanks, submarines, and missile systems.[27] This gravy train will cease to run if Taiwan reunites

---

27 Shirley A. Kan, *Taiwan, Major US Arms Sales since 1990*, Congressional Research Service, August 29, 2014

with China. If China decides to invade Taiwan, are we really willing to intercede on their behalf potentially launching World War III? I for one hope not! Would they come to the aide of the US and fight and die for our freedom? Most assuredly not!

US policy makers cling to the concept of strategic ambiguity to maintain the status quo. Applying this paradigm, our actions and alliances must leave both the Russians and Chinese guessing whether or not the US would take action to maintain the sovereignty of the Ukraine and Taiwan. Strategic ambiguity, however, often results in the unnecessary deaths of tens of thousands. The governments of the Ukraine and Taiwan would behave very differently if not charmed with the illusion of American support. We provide them with weapons to fight and falsely bolster their confidence. When we fail to intercede on their behalf, we will leave them like lambs before the slaughter. The recent policy reversal regarding the Kurds provides an excellent example. For years, the US had supported the Kurdish minority in Iraq and even recruited them to help fight ISIS forces in Syria. A single phone call between the senior leaders of the US and Turkey in 2019 dramatically altered our policy. President Trump agreed to look the other way as Turkish forces crossed into Syria to attack our former Kurdish allies.[28] Imagine the Kurds sense of betrayal. The governments

---

28 Fred Kaplan, Trump's Worst Betrayal Yet, https://slate.com/news-and-politics/2019/10/trump-kurds-world-order-betrayal.html, October 14, 2019.

of the Ukraine and Taiwan should take note—far safer to seek peaceful resolution with their neighbors than to depend upon fickle US support which can turn on a dime. Their domestic problem mirrors ours, however. The Ukrainian and Taiwanese people who will needlessly fight and die are not the same who benefit from the war. Their armed forces are mere pawns on the chessboard willingly sacrificed for the benefit of the "Kings and Queens", aka the ruling political elites.

Regardless of the necessity, the US military establishment has created new threats for which it must now posture to fight. Facing the Chinese and Russians in future full spectrum conflict requires updated warfighting doctrine and weapons. These potential foes have studied the American way of war and patiently watched us grind our swords into plowshares over the last two decades. Politicians of all parties have supported using the US military in peacekeeping operations and surgical strikes by small special operations forces. Our armed forces have thus largely forgotten the art of fighting a peer foe of similar size and capabilities. We stopped worrying about such scenarios after the collapse of the Soviet Union in 1991. Meanwhile, the communists developed weapons and tactics to prevent the US from deploying forces to intervene in the areas of interest— namely Eastern Europe and the waters surrounding China. The US has thus recently developed a military strategy called Multi-Domain Operations or Multi-Domain Ops for short to counter the communists. I call it Multi-Domain Oops! It is perhaps the most intellectually shallow war fighting concept ever developed by the US. This further supports my earlier point regarding the "dumbing down" of our senior military leadership. Allow me to explain.

The Chinese and Russians have developed Anti-Access Area Denial (A2/AD) capabilities to prevent the US from deploying military forces into contested zones. Their weapons and tactics include long-range missiles to destroy our ships and aircraft before they can reach their targets, as well as electronic means to disrupt and deny US communications, networks, and precision navigation. In order to plow through these defenses, Multi-Domain Operations envisions using all Services' capabilities together in a perfectly synchronized fashion and using weapons for multiple roles. A long-range artillery piece originally designed to target enemy ground forces, for instance, could also be used to destroy threat ships. This would require the Navy or intelligence community to share radar or satellite information with the Army artillery unit to provide targeting coordinates and bearing. A very nice vision, but unfortunately, no detailed plan exists to create a robust and secure network to share all of this data. For perspective, the Army has struggled to create a Command and Control network to share data amongst its ground-based air defense systems. This effort was originally launched in 2006 and has since cost the Army nearly $3 Billion and still has not fielded any new equipment to soldiers. The modest achievement to date simply combines two different radars' track data.[29] Sharing data and making centralized command decisions across multiple military weapon systems from all services is far more complex than our leaders can possibly imagine. They are running with scissors and dreaming of technologies they might have seen in the movies but have insufficient technical depth to understand the associated complexities.

Even if the US DoD had a plan to create such a network, as previously stated, both the Chinese and Russians have developed expertise in shutting these down or worse yet, infiltrating and spoofing. Imagine that aforementioned artillery unit mistakenly targeting US ships instead of enemy ships—that would be a bad day made possible by advanced hacking capabilities. As an example, the Russians continue to harass the Ukraine with all types of cyber incursions across the entire spectrum of their society. Andy Greenberg notes:

In Russia's shadow, the decades-old nightmare of hackers stopping the gears of modern society has become a reality. And the blackouts weren't just isolated attacks. They were part of a digital blitzkrieg that has pummeled Ukraine for the past three years—a sustained cyberassault unlike any the world has ever seen. A hacker army has systematically undermined

---

29 US Army, *Army Integrated Air and Missile Defense successfully intercepts test targets*, December 12, 2019. https://www.army.mil/article/230907/army_integrated_air_and_missile_defense_system_successfully_intercepts_test_targets

practically every sector of Ukraine: media, finance, trans-
portation, military, politics, energy. Wave after wave of
intrusions have deleted data, destroyed computers, and in
some cases paralyzed organizations' most basic functions.[30]

There are many other examples of well-developed capabilities to shut down, infiltrate and exploit networks which have multiple access points and customers. Multi-domain operations, therefore, moves the US military in the exact opposite direction needed to ensure our security. We should be developing weapons which can operate autonomously in any environment without relying upon outside information and networks as this makes them vulnerable to cyber-attacks. Our warfighting doctrine must account for the enemy's strengths and the reality of the world today. The enemy gets a vote and they will most assuredly take away our networks, eyes, and ears as these are nearly indefensible assets.

I know you probably think there is no way the US could cling to such an ill-advised military strategy. Surely, we are not this stupid! Unfortunately, we have recently made a very similar grand mistake. In 2006, the US began to lose control in Iraq due to the outbreak of a sectarian civil war between the Sunni and Shia factions. General Petraeus sold President George W. Bush on a new Counterinsurgency strategy, COIN for

---

30 Andy Greenberg, *How an Entire Nation Became Russia's Test Lab for Cyberwarfare*, June 20, 2017, https://www.wired.com/story/russian-hackers-attack-ukraine/

short, which he played the key role in drafting. This involved increasing military forces in Iraq by 40% while moving from a posture of 15 to 21 Brigade Combat Teams on the ground in Iraq.[31] He aimed to calm things down by bringing more military force to bear and using it differently.

The General postulated that COIN is a struggle for the population's support. Understanding that struggle or becoming "the world expert on your district" is the foundation for any [military] unit.[32] In other words, COIN represents a paradigm shift in conventional military thinking. Traditional wisdom holds the enemy as the center of gravity and therefore the focus of military efforts to win. The US armed forces, however, did not possess enough knowledge of the cultural landscape to discern friend from foe. Because of the lack of intelligence and cultural understanding, COIN strategy pragmatically shifted the focus onto the civilian population. But which people are we talking about, the Sunni or the Shia? To help one entity is to de facto hurt the other when they are engaged in a Civil War. Additionally, this strategy did nothing to address the root causes of the strife between the two factions. It is tantamount to a bouncer pushing two belligerents out of the club and into the parking lot. The fight will most assuredly continue outside of the bouncer's

---

31 Frederick W. Kagan, *Understanding General Petraeus's Strategy*, June 27, 2007, The Weekly Standard.
32 Department of the Army, FM 3-4.2: *Counterinsurgency Tactics*, page 1-26, April 2009.

purview. Additionally, the two parties may decide they hate the bouncer more than they hate each other and create a temporary alliance of convenience. A child can see the folly behind COIN doctrine when implemented in a foreign land which rejects the culture of the military occupiers. Nevertheless, nobody else had any answers to the unfolding crisis in Iraq and politicians refused to simply call it a loss and leave Iraq to determine its own fate.

Petraeus provided a roadmap to nowhere and a fundamentally flawed plan. COIN doctrine violates perhaps the most important principle of warfare—simplicity. If we cannot tell our young military personnel exactly what we expect them to do in a combat zone in terms easily understood by all, then shame on our leaders. Eighteen-year-old soldiers on the line lack the education, maturity, and experience, of the senior officers who make grandiose and complex plans. These young warriors, however, are the ones who must stand in the breach and execute hair-brained ideas. We should not expect a young soldier to think and act like a modern-day Lawrence of Arabia capable of navigating the complexities of Middle Eastern tribal cultures. Nobody else had any better ideas, however, and no one wanted to admit we had created an unsolvable conundrum. The slow and inevitable failure of the US to quell violence and bring the conflicts in either Iraq or Afghanistan to a successful conclusion resulted in COIN falling out of favor.[33]

---

33 Karsten Friis, *Can the Counterinsurgency Doctrine be Saved?*, The Diplomat, November 3, 2015.

Unfortunately, the US followed this pseudo-intellectual and flawed strategy for years at great cost in blood and treasure out of political convenience. Nobody had the courage to simply admit we had created a hot mess to which there was no solution. The primary author of the strategy, General Petraeus, suffered no consequences for this failed approach. In fact, just the opposite unfolded. Petraeus retired as a four star and became the Director of the CIA! His political savvy created the bullshit charade necessary to sustain the conflicts and keep the defense dollars flowing. He was thus rewarded appropriately for the futile effort.

When the senior military leaders of our country created Multi-Domain Operations to counter the Red Wave, therefore, we should all rightfully question the underlying logic and motivations. The strategy might just be another way to stoke public paranoia and justify excessively high military spending. In other words, a new way to sustain the routine. How many of the authors of Multi-Domain Operations will soon go to work for defense industry I wonder?

We would all do well to shed our fear of communism and fully open our eyes to the motivations of those who fuel our paranoia. Consider Viet Nam and Cuba. The US lost 58,000 lives and inflicted over a million casualties on our "enemies" in Viet Nam with no effect—the communists won and continue to rule today. Does Viet Nam pose a threat to our democracy and way of life? Absolutely not! They are a peaceful nation with which we have a robust trade relationship. Our relationship with Cuba, on the other hand, remains confrontational to this day because of US efforts to overthrow Fidel Castro and the communist regime. Meanwhile, Cuba continues to thrive just a few hundred miles off our coast. Imagine the healthy trade and tourism exchange we might have had with Cuba for decades if not for our anti-communist bias.

What about the distribution of income? America's ultra-wealthy fear communist tendencies which might see them strung up and flogged to death while the grubby masses claim everything in their pockets. This is what happens in communist countries correct? Money to the communists is like peanut butter to be spread evenly over the collective toast correct? Not really! China now has 819 billionaires, more than any other country in the world![34] The US has 585 in comparison. Russia comes in number five on the list with a total of 96. What happened to the fundamental tenet of communism which promotes power to the people and an equal share of the nation's wealth? These countries are not so different from us after all. Money is power and this ends up concentrating in the hands of a few elites whether in a democratic or a communist nation.

Additionally, let us not forget the fundamental right of self-determination which helped form the ideological bedrock

---

34   James Burton, How Many Billionaires are there in the World, August 29, 2018. https://www.worldatlas.com/articles/how-many-billionaires-are-there-in-the-world.html

of our war of independence from Great Britain. People have the right to decide how they want to be governed without interference from outside entities. Yet we continue to attempt to block rival forms of government abroad and overthrow regimes to satisfy the latest political whims. Our fear of communism is just another patriotic illusion perpetuated by stakeholders who profit from the resulting policies and conflict.

Proposed Reforms

- Challenge intellectual theft in international court and seek wide ranging economic sanctions against perpetrators. Nations which routinely steal commercial and military trade secrets from others must be held accountable. The true nature of the ongoing war involves grand scale theft. These loopholes must be closed. Of course, this also implies if the US is engaged in intellectual property theft, it must cease such operations.

- Stop issuing work and student visas to the citizens of countries knowingly engaged in intellectual property theft.

- Remove all US trade secrets from the internet. Mechanical design diagrams, patents, unique chemical formulae, and all other manner of valuable intellectual property is being harvested on a grand scale from afar. Trusting the security of the internet, even when traffic is encrypted, is akin to having unprotected sex at a brothel in Bangkok. The internet is a vulnerable, modern-day Tower of Babel waiting to crumble under the weight of its complex enormity. When it falls, we best have a back up plan. If not, an irreversible catastrophe will likely unfold—Babylon 2.0.

- Bring China and Russia into the forefront of international security. Assign them responsibilities to help police waters haunted by pirates off the Horn of Africa and peacekeeping roles in places such as the Sinai Peninsula. They must have skin in the game. Both nations benefit from a well-ordered international community and must, therefore, pay some of the costs associated with maintaining it.

- The US must extract itself from entangling alliances and only deploy military personnel and equipment to places which we are serious about defending. The best deterrent to aggression is American boots on the ground. Otherwise, we create false impressions and cause unnecessary violence and death.

- Create a separate, stand-alone, closed-loop network for all critical US infrastructure to include energy, water, agriculture, and major financial markets. When these touch the internet, they can be shut down by our rivals.

CHAPTER 7

Disobedience is Dangerous

The important thing is not to stop questioning.
Curiosity has its own reason for existence.
—Albert Einstein

S HORTLY AFTER RETIRING FROM the Army, I began writing to capture and crystalize lessons learned from my leadership journey. I shared my thoughts and articles with many of my peers and began to develop a reputation as an unconventional thinker in this domain. One of my professional colleagues still in uniform, therefore, asked me to conduct an hour-long professional development session with his core management team. Approximately 15 mid-career Army officers and civilians were present representing over 300 years of collective experience.

I opened the session by asking who in the audience had ever disobeyed an order from a superior officer. The question hung in the air like a stale fart—silence. Unfortunately for the audience, I had played this game before. I refused to move on with the discussion and patiently waited for what seemed an eternity. Still no response. Maybe I had come out of the gates too strong for these wooly creatures. I decided to turn down the heat a little. "Okay, forget disobedience for a moment. Who among you has ever disagreed with a higher authority?" I asked. Disobedience first requires independent thought in order to arrive at a disagreement. Wait for it......crickets! I stared at the crowd in astonishment.

"You have to be kidding me" I responded. "You mean to tell me none of you ever had the courage to disagree with your boss? (I intentionally challenged their self-images by indirectly calling them cowards). Have you never landed in a situation where you were asked or ordered to do something which seemed stupid, illegal, or unnecessarily dangerous?"

This prompted a response from an outspoken combat veteran Lieutenant Colonel. "Sir, I always just assumed my boss had better information than me. Who am I to question the wisdom of higher authority?" The discussion thus began to pick up.

"You mean to tell me you've gone on life and death missions without ever wondering if there was a better way to skin the cat?" I asked.

"Yes Sir!"

A brutally honest Warrant Officer offered "I don't want to risk getting passed over for promotion and not reaching retirement age. I do what I must for the financial security of my family." A very interesting rationalization. He might be unnecessarily killed by following stupid orders but claimed to be worried about his family's financial security. They will be far less secure if he prematurely took a dirt nap.

I marveled at the culture of unconditional obedience to which these leaders unanimously subscribed. Of course, the military emplaces stronger disincentives to disobey or even disagree than most organizations. A military member can be tried by court martial for disobeying an order and spend many years in a Federal prison depending upon the severity of the circumstances. Operational urgency sometimes demands and justifies shutting your mouth and doing what you are told, but such circumstances comprise far less than 1% of a servicemember's career. What about all the other situations where there is time to debate, disagree, and offer alternatives? Unfortunately, even openly disagreeing risks getting shit-canned by your boss on the next evaluation. It only takes one substandard professional report card to end an aspiring officer's career. Couple these powerful forces with the fact that the military attracts some of the most compliant individuals in America and you have a recipe for disaster. Young uniformed professionals are conditioned to turn off their minds, muffle their doubts and simply carry out their orders. In other words, stop leading and just follow. We live in a sheepish world!

Quite tragic and ironic that the military does not truly seek to leverage our individual intelligence as demonstrated by the discussion outlined above. Nevertheless, our wit is the trait which makes us most dangerous! Our ancestors stretching back into antiquity survived predation, wars, famine, and disease not because they were big and strong, but because they were smart. As it applies to our current conflicts, all the dumb terrorists are now dead, weeded out through an accelerated process of natural selection. The board on which we now play is a deadly game of hide and seek. Intelligence will decide who wins our wars, not strength and stamina. Yet the Army stumbles blindly forward incentivizing obedience and developing marketing slogans like "Warriors wanted" in an attempt to resonate with America's youth. These miss the mark. As technology advances, warfare grows ever more complex and technical thus requiring different types of warriors to compliment the traditional knuckle-dragging hulks who kick in doors and shoot people in the face. Good luck with that approach if you do not know the right doors to smash!

The military should begin to measure different types of intelligence (problem solving, emotional, geospatial, raw intelligence quotient, etc.) and use these results to inform promotions and assignments. Every service has a physical fitness test to ensure operational suitability, but none measure intelligence. Army Officers do not even have to take a test to demonstrate specific job knowledge, yet we capture and codify how many pushups they can do. How archaic! An organization will only develop that which it measures and incentivizes. This simple example demonstrates how our armed forces have failed to keep up with the times. Its collective psyche remains locked in the days when physical toughness decided combat outcomes. Yes, a physical component to warfare remains, but mental acuity, cultural and historical awareness, problem solving skills and raw intelligence are now the decisive variables. The military may want warriors, but what it actually needs are nerds who have the intellectual courage to disagree and even disobey with stupid guidance while finding new and better ways to find and stop our enemies

The military, however, does not stand alone when it comes to worshipping obedience. From the time our children exit the womb, we condition them to comply and listen to their parents and elders. As soon as they can take care of their own basic needs and dress themselves, we send them off to school. Here they encounter a hierarchy which also does not tolerate straying from the herd. As we load them onto the bus, we remind them to "do what you are told and pay attention to what the teacher is peddling". In other words, do not spend too much time thinking for yourself. Those rowdy few children prone to disagreement quickly discover time-out, detention, and suspension from school. We thus mold our children who might otherwise be leaders into followers before they even get out of the gates. Turn off your rich internal dialogue in order to simply receive the spoon-fed information.

Nevertheless, having an alert, independent and observant mind is central to survival—particularly for humans as we are relatively frail in comparison to much of the animal kingdom. I would wager, however, that few have ever considered the importance of an inquisitive mind in the context of a crucial leadership quality.

Question: "Why have the woods suddenly become very quiet?"

Answer: There is a dangerous predator nearby.

Question: "Why are animals suddenly behaving erratically?"

Answer: There is a raging wildfire nearby creating a panicked withdraw.

These simple questions demonstrate stopping to ask why keeps us alive and prosperous as individuals. Those who do not pay close attention to their surroundings by continually assessing the environment and asking why are doomed to soon become part of the food chain—or at least this was so in more primitive times. Perhaps modern civilization has short-circuited both natural selection and the advancement of people with the right attributes to serve others. Leaders, however, must remain even more vigilant and inquisitive as they are responsible not only for themselves, but must also mind the welfare of an extended group—no followers, no leader. They therefore have an exponentially greater number of phenomena of concern beyond what is necessary for their individual survival. A leader has higher-level questions to ask that concern the welfare of his subordinates.

Question: "Why are the traditional hunting grounds no longer yielding enough food for the entire tribe?"

Answer: The tribe has grown beyond the capacity for the local environment to sustain and animal populations have dwindled. The tribe must now migrate to find more fruitful lands.

Question: "Why is stored food mysteriously disappearing?"

Answer: One family entrusted to guard the food supply is taking more than its share while everyone else is away from camp.

One can easily see that "why" serves as an essential word in a leader's vocabulary. Possessing an active mind and constantly questioning everything is fundamental to successful leadership, but this does not come without consequences. The brain is the largest and most demanding organ in the body; it consumes approximately 20% of the body's total resources and the more active it is, the more it must be fed. Conserving energy by simply going along and allowing someone else to ask the tough questions and do most of the thinking to defend the collective good serves as an effective survival strategy. It minimizes fatigue and caloric intake requirements. If effective leaders occupy the helm or there are no major threats lurking nearby, the sheep happily keep their heads down and enjoy the pasture; there is either a lion present to protect them, or the predators have gone extinct. Most people are therefore followers who are neither mentally active nor sufficiently concerned about the common good to make capable leaders. Nevertheless, sheep have infiltrated leadership positions across the entire spectrum of American society as wealth, family support, nepotism, and political skill have trumped inquisitiveness and cooperation as leadership prerequisites. Make no mistake, however, crises have come to the fore which require keenly aware and observant lions at the helm; jackals lurk in the shadows.

How do you measure the powers of keen observation? Are the people who get the top grades in school the best suited to lead? Conventional wisdom seems to dictate this because good grades are the most common metric used to gauge whether an individual is prepared for advanced leadership training. Academic excellence is the primary entrance criteria for all military academies and other prestigious institutions of higher learning which fancy themselves leadership factories.

But getting good grades in school only requires regurgitating someone else's wisdom and therefore does not serve as an appropriate leader yardstick. Because grades are easily measured, we use them as screening criteria, but this is simply intellectual laziness; more evidence that sheep rule our everyday lives and preeminent institutions. In fact, those who do well in formal education often do so because they never question what they are being taught; blind faith in the academic altar if you will. A sheep will not waste his energy probing the premises of a theorem, for instance, he will simply memorize the procedures to perform the appropriate mathematical operation. A lion, however, will likely ponder the fundamental theorem of calculus, and perhaps challenge that an infinite number of connected straight lines really can converge to a smooth curve. In struggling with the underlying logic, the lion will come to understand calculus at a much deeper and intuitive level, but in doing so, he may not have sufficiently practiced the mechanical procedures to always arrive at the correct answers on the never-ending series of exams in school. Those who strive for true understanding do not always receive the best grades. Academic excellence does not guarantee intellectual curiosity and vice versa. Recognizing this quality is more of an art than a science—you may struggle to define effective measures for inquisitiveness, but you know it when you see it. Furthermore, those who simply memorize mechanical operations, facts, and figures, do not understand anything at a sufficiently deep level to ever take the next step and plow new intellectual ground. They are only suited for rote tasks required to keep the routine going…. but we put them in charge because they garner the most sheep-defined accolades.

Observing ones' environment and assimilating new knowledge begins with intellectual curiosity. Some of the most profound discoveries of the scientific community are rooted in Newton's struggles, for instance, to discover why objects in motion behave predictably and seem to follow unwritten rules; a finding that most sheep merely take for granted. Every high school science student learns about Newton's laws of motion and gravitation as they have countless useful applications. These are only part of our everyday knowledge because of one uniquely curious human's tenacious series of inquiries. New discoveries always start with someone with the courage to question conventional wisdom and ask "why". Is this quality not at the very heart of changing something in a useful way—also called leadership? Nevertheless, you rarely if ever hear about curiosity in the context of leadership training. Perhaps because it is very difficult to develop and measure, and a quality which would also find high-ranking sheep woefully lacking.

The best leaders anticipate the need to change in order to provide enough reaction time to prevent disaster or alternatively, seize emerging opportunities. While no one has yet developed a time machine or a crystal ball capable of traveling into or seeing the future, paying attention to trends pays dividends. Hyper-observant people are the most likely to sense the changing winds and plan accordingly. This is a key distinguishing feature between leaders and followers.

Leaders question everything, but do not confuse this with a lack of conviction and a solid values-based foundation. Quite the opposite is the case. The person who explores alternatives to conventional wisdom, weighs the relative merits of competing ideas, and then arrives at his or her own conclusions is far more committed and invested than he who merely accepts what his teachers, parents, friends and colleagues believe. Here are examples of how a leader might approach some of life's biggest questions:

- Religion: A person might note there is no direct evidence of a creator in the here and now and this provides justification to explore options to the origins of life and the universe. Various alternatives include:
  - All of what we can ever know has been created by a higher being.
  - Everything has simply always existed. The Universe has no beginning, no end, and life has always thrived. Our understanding of time is incomplete because everything we know on Earth has a beginning and end.
  - Life sprang from random collisions of organic molecules. Single cells subsequently grew to ever-increasing levels of complexity while striving to adapt to varying environments.
  - Everything to include life sprang into existence at the outset of the Universe—call it the big bang or the spoken word of a creator.
  - There is no real distinction between living things and non-living objects. The differences in the observed level of complexity between a human and a hydrogen atom is relative to our human scale of reference. A simple atom, for instance, may be infinitely complicated at a level we simply are not equipped to observe because of our size—it could be a universe unto itself or alternatively a life form which we simply cannot recognize.

- Science: Technological progress has greatly improved human existence, but can it provide the answers to fundamental questions such as how the universe and life were created?

  - At a fundamental level, life uses energy to maintain order but science claims that everything in nature tends towards greater disorder—chaos/entropy theory. All phenomena we observe in the natural world point to ever increasing simplicity. Complex molecules break down into more simple components. How do you reconcile this with the theory of life springing into existence and spontaneously generating very sophisticated constructs? Life violates entropy theory, but why and how remain a mystery.

  - Given that science is built upon inductive reasoning, can it ever lead to absolute truth? Science can only say a theory holds true under situations and conditions which a human can observe and test, but are we able to detect all phenomena of relevance across the entire universe? Is it possible that outer space for instance is not a void but simply a substance which humans do not have the senses to detect? Earthworms do not have eyes and therefore cannot detect or understand visible light and other electromagnetic radiation. What phenomena are humans blind to due to our biological limitations and the confines imposed by planet Earth? What does this possibility mean regarding the conclusions reached by science?

Whether you gravitate towards science or religion for the answers to the tough questions outlined above such as the meaning of life, and the origins of all we observe is a matter of personal preference. If you have not struggled with the issues and questions above, however, you probably do not really believe anything at all and are therefore probably not fit to lead.

A career soldier and officer should also wrestle with the relative merits of American society and government as these are the ostensible reasons for which we fight. In fact, anyone who aspires to serve the public in any capacity should ponder these as well. Some might even argue that you cannot be a responsible citizen or voter without understanding your stance on these matters.

- Government:
  - Is representative democracy the optimal form of government? If so, how is it better than direct democracy, communism, socialism, monarchies, and benevolent dictatorships? What are the relative pros and cons? Does the American system need to be modified to account for cultural and technological evolution?
  - What should our laws be based upon? At what point are individual liberties trumped by the needs of the common good?
  - What minimum goods and services should the government provide versus the private sector? What is the

relationship between the form of government and the basis of the economy? What measures (if any) should government emplace to protect its citizens from unfettered capitalism?

— Did the United States spring to superpower status as a result of liberal democracy and capitalism or did the exploitation of the North American continent, its indigenous population, and subsequent waves of slaves and vulnerable immigrants leapfrog us ahead? Does exploitation continue today?

• The Military:

— Is the United States worth defending with your life? How much are you willing to be away from home and your family in defense of your country? If you give all of your time and energy in the pursuit of freedom, are you truly free? Who sacrifices more, the soldier or the family who must provide unconditional support without receiving any recognition or compensation?

— When, if ever, is it okay to kill non-combatants in the pursuit of your enemies?

— How do you define a terrorist? Do domestic gangs and extremist groups qualify under your definition? If so, should we leverage military resources to defeat these people?

— What are the root causes of terrorism against the United States? Are current military operations and strategies addressing these causal forces?

- Is it okay to indefinitely intern terrorists with no trial or due process?
- Should the United States be in the business of regime change using military force?
- When should a soldier disobey an order?
- When is it okay to disagree with a superior officer?

There are many other options to explore as well; the questions above merely provide insight into the mind of an inquisitive person who takes nothing for granted. If you have not struggled with finding truth in such a fashion than you may not really believe in anything at all; you simply take a host of very important issues for granted. If you trust in a kind creator, for instance, and have not balanced that against your life experiences, when personal tragedy strikes close to home, you may be prone to abandon your faith. The person, who has struggled with these issues ahead of time and knows life is not always fair but believes in a benevolent creator, nonetheless, will not suffer such an ideological upheaval. Questioning everything is central to having a solid values-based foundation on which to stand when making difficult decisions; this is widely recognized as an essential leadership trait. One must have a basis for making complex decisions which have no clear correct answer. Committing to principles requires courage and makes you a leader of character. One must never support an issue he has not questioned—that would be blind faith or call it sheepish behavior if you will.

I can only claim expertise in military matters given my extensive experience in this domain. I believe killing to defend yourself, your family, and your country is sometimes necessary and justified but should not be taken lightly. Ending a human life is serious business and should be a measure of last resort! I do not believe we should ever fight for someone or another country not willing to fight for themselves; this only results in temporary gains at best. I believe military occupation of foreign lands breeds hatred much as the British occupation of the colonies fueled the American revolution. I believe the root cause of terrorism against the United States is hatred and our policies of killing and occupying foreign territory are not an effective treatment for this ailment. In fact, we are probably less safe now than we were 18 years ago when we launched the Global War on Terror given the terrible loss of life we have inflicted and devastation we have wrought across the world. Finally, I believe we desperately need to change our military approach to ensuring our National security but the individuals responsible for leading this are sheep who only know how to sustain the current never-ending cycle of violence.

Much conventional leadership wisdom speaks to the need for common sense (which is not very common as it turns out). There is a strong correlation between an inquisitive mind and common sense. The person who takes time to think about things for themselves is much less likely to be stumped by common pitfalls which trap others who take much for granted. Intellectual laziness is the most crippling form of sloth; life is hard, but it is harder when you are stupid. The sheep of the world, however, squarely fall into the camp of "ignorance is bliss".

Leaders must always seek the truth; you cannot make sound decisions without the best information possible. The individual with an inquisitive mind is better equipped to get to the bottom of complex issues given his predisposition to constantly question everything. One word of caution. A leader should never openly question a subordinates' motives or capability as he will forever alienate this person by embarrassing him in front of his coworkers. One senior leader for whom I worked routinely responded to subordinates by saying "Thanks for the information: it is mildly interesting, but totally irrelevant". This was his way of saying the subordinate was missing the point, but it engendered great resentment in the ranks; particularly so because he was a General Officer. There is never a need to insult people when seeking the truth. A leader needs the cooperation of his subordinates to understand what is occurring in the trenches. Metaphorically shooting them in the face for offering their insights serves no positive purpose and will only chill the waters and discourage other key personnel from providing input.

Leading with questions is an art form which becomes ever more important as a person climbs through the ranks into positions of significant influence. As soon as the leader takes a stance on an issue by making firm statements or pushing opinions, all learning and collaboration will likely grind to a halt. Asking questions on the other hand displays humility and a willingness to listen and learn. It also builds teamwork; when executed correctly, the leader promotes a learning culture by encouraging everyone with a dog in the fight to ask questions in the pursuit of the truth or best solution to a problem. Heated debate and dialogue are healthy when based upon mutual respect and trust. Subordinates must trust their leader will not hold a grudge for delivering contradictory advice and the leader must in turn trust subordinates will loyally execute his guidance after having the opportunity to provide input. Establishing this organizational culture of excellence begins with the leader's inquisitive mind and often requires leaders to listen more than they speak.

Continuously asking why also promotes a better understanding of the people within your organization; one of your paramount responsibilities. Leaders sometimes rush to judgement and punitive action when subordinates get off track, but how many first ask why and seek the root cause of the transgression? In some cases, there simply is no excuse so to speak and negative action is in order. In others, however, the organization and perhaps even the leader failed the subordinate. Did the individual in question have the time, the tools, and the training required to accomplish their duties (a good first question for every leader)? If not, why not? Perhaps the organization needs better on-boarding procedures and a mentoring program to prevent people from falling through the cracks. The inquisitive leader sees the organization at a deeper level and will come to understand

and therefore be able to positively influence individual behaviors and the associated outcomes. Never stop asking why.

Digging into issues is an important leader quality as demonstrated above, but it does not come without consequences. Any suck-up can comply with higher authority. Blind obedience avoids the risk of professional reprisals and does not require the effort to think for oneself. Compliance is safe and what good followers practice. It takes a leader and strongly independent person, however, to muster the courage to disagree or disobey. Sadly, we devote precious little energy to the topic and every culture emplaces strong incentives to simply go along to get along. We do not even address this issue in strictly academic settings. Our schools do not discuss when to disobey as educators benefit from controlled compliance. Why would they teach children to question authority when chaos might result? The vignette below, however, vividly demonstrates the need to reconsider this approach.

In 1983, Stanislav Petrov, a Lieutenant Colonel in the Soviet air defense forces, served as a duty officer responsible for monitoring the nuclear readiness of the United States. During his watch, a newly deployed Soviet early warning satellite constellation malfunctioned and falsely reported the US had launched a preemptive nuclear strike. Other Soviet battle command systems initially corroborated a US Intercontinental Ballistic Missile (ICBM) attack was in fact underway and it was up to Stanislav to initiate the sequence of events for a Soviet response. The situation did not make sense, however, and he resisted great pressure from higher authority to fulfill his duties in accordance with predetermined rules of engagement. When the purported ICBMs came within range of ground-based Soviet air defense radars and failed to appear, it soon became apparent the US had not launched an attack after all. Had Petrov immediately complied with standard rules of engagement and lawful orders from his commanders, the world might have ended in the flames of thousands of nuclear weapons. Unfortunately, Stanislav Petrov received neither accolades nor a promotion from the Soviet military; his career ended unceremoniously. No society, east or west, values disobedience. Never mind the very fate of the world sometimes hinges upon such courageous action.

In an age of rising military tension between the US and its nuclear-armed peer competitors Russia and China, we must ask ourselves, are US military leaders willing to disobey under circumstances similar to Petrov's dilemma? Various perspectives exist on this matter, but consider for a moment the actual incentives, rules, and regulations under which US military members operate. The Uniform Code of Military Justice (UCMJ) serves as the legal framework for all soldiers, sailors, airmen, and marines. Curiously, a service member can be punished for disobeying a lawful order under the UCMJ (Article 92), but there is no such punishment for issuing illegal orders. All the responsibility for determining whether or not an order is legal, therefore, lies with the subordinate who is junior both in rank and experience to his boss. The senior issuing an illegal directive enjoys impunity under the UCMJ and also holds the fate of the subordinates' career in his hands through the power of the pen. In addition to the authority to invoke UCMJ upon subordinates, commanders also control their career progression. As previously mentioned, one substandard performance evaluation immediately halts any future promotion for military personnel. Bucking authority, therefore, rarely ends well. Even disagreement, a watered-down prelude to disobedience, becomes difficult for uniformed personnel operating under the constraints of both a regulatory framework and hierarchical command structure stacked against them. Obedience reigns supreme in the military domain. While many military leaders proclaim the value of "out of the box" thinking, the incentive structure prevents such individuals from rising through the ranks—get your asses back in the box if you want to succeed.

The US Department of Defense would do well to remedy this situation and begin to hold senior leaders accountable for their orders. Any military official who knowingly issues an illegal directive has lost their moral compass and has no business leading America's sons and daughters. Deciding the propriety of military orders cannot be left solely to subordinates who suffer all the consequences under the current framework.

This action alone, however, is insufficient. All military personnel need better training and education on when, why, and how to disobey. Many cannot even tell you which laws they are required to obey. Do all international laws and agreements such as the Geneva and Hague accords apply all of the time? Do the laws of host nations apply when they contradict US criminal and civil law and the UCMJ? These are important questions with serious consequences.

Additionally, the crisis outlined above vividly demonstrates refusing to obey only illegal orders is woefully inadequate. Other circumstances surely exist where a service member should disobey. Do orders that are simply dumb or will likely result in unnecessary loss of life or property damage merit consideration for disobedience? If not, what is your personal litmus test? Do you even have one? If you have not considered these issues, you may call yourself a leader, but you are more likely a swift running lemming blindly following a leader headed towards the cliff. Hopefully, you will not have your fingers on the red button on a day similar to Stanislav's dilemma in 1983.

Military and civilian authorities must explore complex legal and moral dilemmas before they land in our laps catching us ill-prepared. If we hide behind military or organizational urgency and say nay, a subordinates' job is to simply execute directives with enthusiasm, how will you react when you learn someone you love died unnecessarily in the name of obedience? Is it possible, for instance, that the absence of alternatives to stale approaches to conflict resolution result from a culture of obedience? Why risk contradicting the status quo when it will only result in your personal demise? A real leader does not have to ask this question. In light of this discussion, ask yourself if those we have entrusted with the reins of power deserve their positions. Contrary to conventional wisdom, conformance not disobedience, poses the greatest threat to our security and way of life!

Proposed Reforms

- Formal disobedience training for all school age youth. Children need to understand that it is okay to disagree and even disobey. They also need coaching on how and when to do this. We all must carefully think through situations which demand us to take a stand. Given the growing awareness of sexual predators, for instance, we have taught our children to disobey people in positions of authority who might aim to hurt them. This is a positive development, but woefully insufficient. Many circumstances exist which demand disobedience. If you take a moment to think about it, the only times we have made positive and necessary reforms are when millions of Americans decided to disobey.

- Implement enhanced measures to protect individuals who disobey with illegal, immoral, or stupid guidance from reprisals. Whistle-blower protections provide a good example. The military must add a new clause under the Uniform Code of Military justice to punish senior officers for issuing illegal and inappropriate orders. All the responsibility should not rest on the subordinate's shoulders while risking life, limb, and career to stand against tyrannical superiors.

CHAPTER 8

Democracy trumps Corruption

The government you elect is the government you deserve.
—Thomas Jefferson

I STARED AT MY DIMLY lit computer screen trying to find a pattern in the seemingly random logistical data. It was 2010 and we were trying to move mountains of defense equipment out of Iraq. The US called it the responsible drawdown of forces. Military operations in Iraq were winding down and the Army sought to transition security and peacekeeping responsibilities over to the Iraqis. We needed to move some two million steel shipping containers and tens of thousands of military vehicles from over 300 Forward Operating Bases (FOBs) scattered across the country. The vast majority of equipment needed to be moved by heavy, flatbed trucks via a patchwork of roads in various states of disrepair between Iraq and Kuwait. Once in Kuwait, the equipment would be refurbished and sent to either Afghanistan or back to the US.

Our initial efforts met with much armed resistance and a never-ending series of Improvised Explosive Devices (IEDs). Many diverse factions attacked US convoys and casualties began to mount. Additionally, mountains of equipment began to pile up in enormous property redistribution lots the size of mega-shopping malls. Our prospects of salvaging the billions of dollars of equipment looked grim until we changed our strategy. Why not leverage Iraqi shipment companies to move our equipment? We thus contracted with local Iraqi sheiks who leveraged their indigenous connections to get the convoys through to Kuwait undamaged. One of my jobs was to predict when the property redistribution yards would be full enough to justify hiring an Iraqi convoy. These mammoth assemblies of trucks could stretch for miles when parked bumper to bumper. If US forces could not fully load them up immediately, we stood to lose millions of dollars per day to keep the vehicles and drivers on hold. Timing the arrival of the convoys was crucial. In working with the Sheiks, I came to understand the concept of "baksheesh" or bribe money. In order to get the convoys safely through, every local warlord, chief, or sheik presiding over a particular region expected tribute—also known as baksheesh. This tax if you will, is a common and culturally acceptable way of doing business in the Middle East.

We Americans look down our noses at such overtly corrupt practices, but how different are we? One of the more educated sheiks helped me see our respective systems through different eyes. He articulated that baksheesh stands in the light of day and everyone pays the same tax, no secrets, no surprises. A very fair and egalitarian way of doing business from his foxhole. In his opinion, Americans also pay business taxes to get their way, but they are in the dark and nobody is really quite certain who is paying whom—in the US we call them bribes. What is fairer, a system understood and accessible to all or a system where only the ultra-wealthy are able to influence power brokers through under the table bribes and campaign contributions? However you chose to answer this question matters not. The Iraqis and Afghanis, among others, find baksheesh an acceptable way of doing business and reject our principles. Who are we to tell them otherwise? Corruption lies in the eyes of the beholder and exists within a specific cultural context.

Since the time we were children in America, we have been taught to believe democracy is the best and most incorruptible form of government. Elected officials must answer to the people or risk getting booted out of office. Everyone has a voice through the power of the ballot box. We were also founded on the belief that nobody is above the law and early American colonists rejected the royal families who ruled across Europe at the birth of our nation. These monarchies concentrated both wealth and political power in the hands of a very few. Ask yourself, how different is the US today? Wealth and power have both become generational—we operate not so differently from medieval times where family titles dominated. Also recall that American democracy institutionalized slavery, failed to recognize women as citizens for over 100 years, and promulgated discriminatory Jim Crow laws. Democracy obviously neither provides a guarantee that human rights will be observed nor guards against corruption. It merely codifies, validates, and normalizes the values of its people. If greed, corruption, racism, and self-indulgence prevail within the population, elected officials will quite naturally reflect these same qualities. Does this resonate with the current state of our union?

Consider this reality in light of American foreign policy decisions. Why do we push so hard to establish democracy in places which do not reflect our values? In regions which hate the United States, democracy guarantees the rise of governments hostile to ours. Pushing our chosen form of government is counter-productive to the desired outcome of standing up nations friendly to ours. Democracy in a region dominated by Muslims, for instance, may result in the "dreaded" establishment of a caliphate government led by fundamental Islamists. The American military fears such a development as conventional wisdom dictates this would result in state sponsored terrorism not so different than Iran. This lies at the heart of our conflict with the Islamic State of Iraq and Syria or ISIS for short. The religion of the people of any particular nation, however, does not necessarily dictate policy. As already discussed, American meddling in Iran, previously friendly to the US, resulted in long term animosity which endures to this day. Their anti-US policy has little or nothing to do with their religion or form of government. It is merely a reaction to our interference in their domestic politics. Fast forward to today, and we pursue a very similar approach in Syria. We are backing those who hope to overthrow the government led by Assad. There are two levels of uncertainty involved here: 1) What policy approach does Assad take towards the US if he is not overthrown? and 2) If Assad loses, who replaces him and how do we know they will be any better? Even if Syria becomes democratic, it remains highly unlikely that any good comes of this war for the American people.

Interesting and highly hypocritical that US military leaders obsess regarding the possible emergence of a caliphate. Outside looking in, we appear to be the Christian States of America from the point of view of many Muslim citizens in the countries we occupy. A non-Christian has never served as our President. At inauguration, the President is sworn in by placing a hand on a bible. We have many references to Christianity in the public realm (take the pledge of allegiance and our currency for instance). Additionally, our laws, culture and founding principles are clearly Christian based. From our enemies' point of view, we are a Christian-based society launching another round of Crusades.

Further fanning these flames, many senior American military leaders are closet evangelists. As a young officer, I was quietly pressured into joining the Officer's Christian

Fellowship or OCF for short. The OCF begins to recruit early and has a strong presence at our military academies. This organization's mission is to "engage military leaders in Biblical fellowship and growth to equip them for Christlike service at the intersection of faith, family, and profession".[35] The very first question one of my new Commander's asked me upon his arrival to our unit was the church at which I worshipped. A curious top priority by my way of thinking—religion, not training, morale, or equipment readiness. He went out of his way to let everyone know he belonged to the OCF. This same Commander later began to hold Bible Study classes at his house every Friday with all of his subordinate officers who chose to participate. I was the only officer in the unit who did not play along with these reindeer games. It seemed inappropriate to me. Imagine the predicament a non-Christian officer in this unit would have faced. This Commander also mandated that our Chaplain lead all our paratroopers in a Christian prayer before making a parachute jump. He liked to say, "there are no atheists at the end of a static line". The static line opens the types of parachutes most often used in military operations. Once again, I was the sole naysayer and refused to force this on my soldiers. In my opinion, religion has no place in our formations. It is a strictly private matter, especially for senior leaders. As soon as you overtly proclaim a particular belief structure or worse yet, begin to proselytize, everyone of a

---

35 Officer's Christian Fellowship homepage, https://www.ocfusa.org/

different faith than you may feel you will discriminate against them. Leader's must be ambassadors of fairness who stand above even the appearance of favoritism.

Fast-forward one year later, and we received a new, higher-level Commander who was also a member of the OCF. I began to marvel at the prevalence and widespread influence of this organization. At the first in briefing with subordinates, this senior leader proudly proclaimed while holding the actual book "The first thing you need to know about me is that I'm a bible thumping Christian." The audience reacted with loud applause and many "hooahs". I wonder if he had said "The first thing you need to know about me is that I'm a Koran thumping Muslim" if the reaction would have been the same? Most assuredly not! Nobody in the audience had either a prayer carpet or knew to face Mecca. I privately squirmed and thought this proclamation highly unprofessional. The Army did not see it the same way, however. This man eventually wore three stars on his collar and overtly cultivated the careers of droves of other OCF members for decades. Yes America, evangelism is alive and well in the ranks of your military. You need to know this because these same senior leaders influence the course of our wars. While nobody in uniform or in the media overtly proclaims we are fighting to promote the spread of Christianity, those forces continue to exert an invisible influence. Separation of Church and State sounds great, but in a Christian-dominated democratic majority, there is no stripping away the influence of religion. We should expect no different in other corners of the world. When subjected to close scrutiny, our overt desire to promote secular governments abroad is highly hypocritical.

Regarding the various possible forms of government, none can exist in the absence of an economic surplus. There must be an excess of goods and services changing hands for a government to tax and subsequently fund itself. No budget, no democracy. Consider this fundamental in light of the American experience in Afghanistan, an extremely primitive land dominated by self-subsistence. It is a goat-based economy where most people struggle to merely survive. Trying to give them democracy, therefore, utterly fails. Most Americans probably do not realize that US taxpayer dollars completely fund the Afghan government and security forces with no end in sight. Poppy production remains the only element of the Afghan economy which thrives despite over 18 years of American intervention, assistance, and tens of billions of dollars cash infusion. Further complicating this hopeless effort is an ancient patchwork tribal network not so different than the over 570 Native American tribes of North America prior to European colonization. Even in the face of genocide, Native Americans rarely cooperated against the constant westward pressure of the settlers. This same tribal competition paradigm exists in Afghanistan today. Given their long-standing cultural animosity and strife with neighboring communities, it is shear folly to expect Afghanis to cooperate and form a single centralized government. Some may call it American arrogance.

Let us return to the foundational principle of "no one above the law". Our constitution provides wiggle room for politicians who might break the rules while executing their duties and this seems reasonable, but how far can they go? It would seem our system has degenerated to a point far past the original intent of the founders. High level officials launching investigations against political rivals is a step too far. What about the power of the pardon being used to protect personal and professional colleagues? Also overboard in my opinion. How about high crimes? If a senior government official knowingly discloses Top Secret information to unauthorized foreign entities with impunity, does this not defy your sensibilities? By the way, the definition of Top Secret is information which if disclosed to unauthorized people could cause EXCEPTIONALLY GRAVE damage to the national security of the United States. Many lower-level people have gone to jail for a very long time for committing such offenses. They also earn the ignominious labels of spy and traitor. A one-time accident is one thing which we might reasonably forgive, but deliberate and repeated transgressions which were hid from oversight is quite another.

Consider justice for the fabulously wealthy who cannot claim public service exemptions. Do you feel they receive equal treatment under the law? Of course not! Money buys special favors and greases the skids with elected officials despite the accountability offered by the ballot box. Most citizens are too busy to concern themselves with the day to day affairs of our justice system, so it fails us at all levels. Anyone who closely follows the Jeffrey Epstein case, for instance, must marvel at how he dodged prosecution for decades in the face of over-whelming evidence. He left a trail of dozens if not hundreds of victims. He had the ultimate wild card however—his pedophile clientele included many very rich, politically connected individuals. In order to protect themselves and remain in the dark, these power brokers undoubtedly had him murdered in his jail cell before he could rat them out. Mysteriously, his cell mate was moved at the last minute, both cameras surveilling his cell area malfunctioned, and the on-duty correctional officers failed to do their routine checks the night he died. Probably not a coincidence. Once again, democracy and justice fail in the face of money, bribes, and campaign contributions. If it requires millions of dollars to run a successful campaign, that money has to come from somewhere. Nobody is interested in handing out free chicken, so the donors get favors in return.

Capitalism is deeply intertwined with our democracy; we cannot easily detangle the two. Our economic model dictates the government should take a relatively hands-off, laissez faire approach to business and let the invisible hand of market forces self-regulate. But what happens when private corporations slowly and imperceptibly become more powerful than our elected officials and collective government? Here are some of the roles and endeavors in which private corporations have already or will soon undertake:

- Develop and distribute their own currency. Crypto currencies such as Bitcoin enable transactions to unfold with little or no government oversight. In some cases, such "made up" currencies undoubtedly help entities who wish to fly below the radar. Crypto currencies will also eventually compete with national-level currencies. Those who control the flow of money control the world. Wealthy individuals, therefore, not elected officials will hold much of the power.

- Raise, train, and equip private armies. Imagine heavily armed corporate security details intervening in places such as Africa where there are no strong centralized governments. Do they have the right to seize whatever resources they may and prop up regimes which support their business?

- Control the resources necessary to survive. When a crisis causes global supply chains to shut down, governments are left powerless. Mega-corporations then step in to fill the power vacuum and provide life's necessities to people in distress.

- Own major media outlets and control the information citizens consume, therefore, exerting considerable influence. Private ownership of social media outlets also enables tight control of messaging. The fabulously wealthy owners get to censor speech and prevent dialogue which might harm them from going viral.

Is there really a distinction between wealth and political power? I do not think so, but it makes a nice bedtime story. If we continue to allow unbounded wealth beyond imagination to accumulate in a very few powerful hands, we effectively put them behind the steering wheel of both our economy and what we view as traditional roles of government. Imagine a fictional mega-corporation called "Ameri-next" with an annual budget greater than the US federal government. If current trends continue, such a future will come to pass. Excessive wealth in the hands of sometimes less than noble individuals with no public accountability will threaten our democracy and way of life.

Proposed Reforms

- Implement additional tax brackets. The Internal Revenue Service currently implements seven tax rates from 10% to 37% depending upon one's taxable income. The top rate (37%) applies to every dollar over approximately $500,000 for a single head of household. Take the case of a small business owner who earns $750,000 per year and is striving to expand. Compare this to a person who earns over $750,000,000 (1000 times more than the small business owner). They both pay the same rate on their income in excess of the $500,000 threshold. This should violate your sense of fairness. The other six rates are implemented at various taxable income thresholds in a graduated fashion. This approach acknowledges that people are more able to pay as they walk up the income ladder. The wealthy also disproportionately benefit from America's economic construct and must pay their fair share.

- Establish a third major political party to provide options at the ballot box. The American two-party system is failing us and often results in a "lesser of two evils" choice come time to vote.

- Provide public funding for the leading candidate of every party. Campaign spending must be closely audited and restricted to the public funds.

- Every candidate must open their financial books and submit to a full audit which outlines the sources and extent of their wealth. These results should be published in major media outlets for all to see.

- Private citizens should watch what candidates do with their personal wealth to help others. We must demand leaders who are interested in improving our world and helping others succeed. This is a far better moral litmus test than listening to their promises about what they intend to do with other people's money: aka your tax dollars. Keep your eyes on their wallets, not their lips.

- Modify the US Constitution to remove the power of the President to pardon people who commit Federal crimes. This power is being used for personal gain.

CHAPTER 9

The American Dream

Keep away from small people who try to belittle your ambitions. Small people always do that, but the really great make you feel that you too can become great.

—Mark Twain

MOST EVERY PARENT WANTS the best possible life for their children. People struggling to merely get by, in particular, want to believe that anything is possible in America. While they may not even have all of life's basic necessities, the expectation of a better future keeps struggling families moving forward. Every poor and hungry child can recall a parent whispering in their ear at bedtime, "you can be anything you want to be—this is America". Food nourishes the body but just as importantly, hopes and dreams sustain the soul.

The promise of the American dream, however, means different things to different people. Some are thankful for the safety and security of living within our borders free from religious or ethnic persecution. Others take a more materialistic view and point at the opportunity to own property, have a nice house with a two-car garage, and send our children to well-resourced schools. While all these aspects of life in the United States are true, the essence of the American dream for me is being born in a place where my dreams themselves are limited only by my imagination and audacity. The "turkey in every pot" mantra rings hollow; the ability to dream BIG is much more rewarding! In my case, I dreamed of being a military professional from a very young age even though nobody in my immediate family had ever served and there were precious few positive role models in sight. Soldiers were and still are my heroes.

Like too many others from disadvantaged backgrounds, however, the idealism of my youth gave way to wildness in my formative teen years. Without structure and a positive vision for the future (call it a dream), I simply went feral. Two years out of high school, I was down on my luck barely scraping by as a temporary hire in a machine shop and beginning to flirt with alcohol abuse. I had no passion for anything except pursuing a "good time" and was deeply angry and frustrated. Luckily, I remembered the long-dormant dream of being a soldier and wandered into the local recruiter's office before I had committed any serious errors. A few months later,

I graduated from basic training and shipped out to West Germany for duty as a border patrolman. I thrived in the presence of structure, discipline, and positive role models and began to realize untapped potential. My leaders took notice, and two years after enlisting, I was headed to West Point. That is when I really began to dream big. If I could go from being a high school loser and anonymous worker on a factory floor to the hallowed halls of the United States Military Academy, why couldn't I be a General someday? After graduating, this very ambitious dream sustained me for over two decades, but alas, I ultimately fell short of the goal after significant sacrifice, trials, and tribulations.

So I asked myself a few years after retiring, was I a failure? Was the Army a waste of my time and talents? Were my dreams too big? It sure did not feel that way. What I have come to realize is that *HAVING A DREAM* is the real prize while achieving it is a distant second place at best. The gratification one feels from obtaining something whether it be wealth or a promotion, for instance, is always short-lived. People are meant to solve problems, overcome, climb, and dream in the same way predators are meant to hunt. The capacity to dream of a better future is a uniquely human trait; it is perhaps the essence of our species. Striving to do something, create something, or become something is what we are here to do. This is probably why many millionaire lottery winners are so unhappy. They have stopped dreaming and effectively become overfed predators apathetically staring at a mountain of meat with no purpose in life but to eat and defecate. The thrill truly is in the chase.

Looking back, I realize how lucky I was to find my way as a soldier and rediscover the passion of my youth. This happened more by accident than by design. I also learned that life is a team sport and developed many rich and rewarding relationships along the way. The dream of becoming a senior Army leader put the pep in my step, the twinkle in my eye, and gave me a passion for my professional life that I would never trade for a more complacent career—sunk costs be damned! When you struggle mightily to achieve a dream and fall short, you simply need a new dream. Upon retirement, therefore, I set new goals which had nothing to do with military service. I leveraged the considerable skills and experiences gained while in uniform to launch a small business and become my own boss. I knew I needed new prey to chase or I would soon have an unhappy, shallow existence. The hunt continues....

The most incredible gift we have is the ability to dream and if you are reading this, you too were fortunate to have been born under circumstances which do not limit you. Now is an excellent time to take stock of your humanity. What are your dreams and what are you doing to chase them? How are you helping others achieve theirs? Cynics and critics never build or accomplish anything of enduring value. There is nothing more important for our long-term success as a civilization, therefore, than to create a culture which encourages and promotes dreamers. It is the most human thing we can do!

Given my upbringing, I was fortunate that my dreams were not forever extinguished at a young age. Unfortunately, untold millions of children in the US are not so lucky. Far too many grow up without hope for a brighter future. In order to restore the American dream for all, we must overcome the negative cycles of generational poverty and systemic racism. Leaders must help young people develop and pursue achievable dreams.

The kernel of any dream should revolve around a person's unique talents and individuality. Everyone possesses special qualities which are waiting to blossom if only planted in the right soil. Unfortunately, our formal education process from kindergarten through high school often handicaps young people. We rack and stack them against three primary criteria: 1) how well they do on formal tests, 2) athletic ability, and 3) popularity. These provide the framework by which school officials and young people judge both themselves and others. Imagine the unfortunate child who does not fare well in any of these domains. He or she is likely to develop a negative self-image and believe they will be condemned to an unfortunate life; especially if born into poverty. How could they possibly escape the circumstances of their birth without doing well in school-defined metrics of success? This too often becomes a self-fulfilling prophecy. While we cannot deny the importance of these three areas, there are so many other qualities which we can think of as superpowers. Nobody, for instance, gets grades for kindness, cooperation, curiosity, musical aptitude, artistic talents, mechanical capability, human and emotional intelligence and so many more special traits. Yet a person can build a positive vision for the future, call it a dream, around any of these amazing attributes. Just because you cannot quantify and measure an attribute does not make it any less important or special. Our educators and guidance counsellors throughout the depth of our system must take an individual approach to encouraging young people in pursuit of a passion leveraging their unique talents. The one-size fits all sheepish approach to educational development must end.

Interestingly, we use the three aforementioned criteria to identify and further develop blossoming leaders. Those who gain admission into military academies, our premier leadership development institutions, must jump through a near endless series of school-centric hoops. High standardized test scores, great grade point averages, participation in multiple sports and extracurricular activities all are a must. If not present, do not even bother applying. Despite conventional wisdom, ask yourself if these achievements correlate with leadership ability? My 35 years of experience does not support this thesis. The real heart of leading requires thinking for oneself. Getting high grades, awesome test scores and achieving amazing feats on the athletic fields, however, do not necessarily require independent thought. Our formal education system actually encourages mere memorization—the ability to accurately recite what someone else thought or mindlessly apply an equation developed centuries ago without questioning its relevance today. Challenging conventional thinking can bog you down because the list of facts, figures, and equations we expect our young people to know keeps growing. Those who mindlessly jump on the bus and do everything their parents, teachers, and coaches demand inevitably emerge as our superstars.

My experiences while teaching environmental science and engineering at West Point opened my eyes to the startling inability of many our nations' best and brightest to think through intricate problems for themselves. Solving environmental issues requires the integration of many scientific disciplines while incorporating the impacts of politics, risks to human health, and cultural values. There are no quick and easy canned answers to spit back at the professor. For instance, how much should we spend to improve drinking water quality if we know current contaminant levels contribute to 10,000 excess American deaths from cancer every year? How would your answer to this question change if those 10,000 deaths all occurred in the wealthy suburbs versus poor inner cities? Even if you believe global warming is happening, what actions can the US take to alter its course when the developing world will likely ignore regulating its emissions? When posing such questions to the class, the vast majority of cadets glazed over like hogs staring at a wristwatch. They simply had no framework to get their arms around such problems because the previous 14+ years of formal education did not require them to truly think for themselves. The most ambitious cadets, however, would constantly seek additional instruction during my non-classroom office hours. These sessions oftentimes entertained. Those struggling to maintain high grades and top-class rank adopted a siege approach to mining out the right answers. They must have felt if they pestered me long enough, I would eventually tell them what I thought about such matters as this was undoubtedly the key to success in their minds. All I demanded, however, was that they think for themselves and logically defend a position supported by quantitative data where available.

The cadets who most often surprised with outstanding answers were middle of the pack type young people who were more familiar with struggling with material than those we usually deem the class leaders. This disconnect contributes to the wrong types of people rising to the top. We cannot judge who best to lead if we do not even recognize the most important attribute—the ability to think for oneself. How many such cadets today are actually chasing their parent's dreams and not their own? Regardless, they will undoubtedly rise to positions of significant influence given the pipeline into which they have inserted themselves. On the other end of the spectrum, how many disenfranchised young people with amazing potential will never rise because of the circumstances of their birth? The leadership crisis playing out on many stages across the US, therefore, correlates with limited and conditional access to the American dream.

Proposed Reforms

- Implement tests which gauge an individuals' ability to think for themselves. These should not depend upon previous knowledge or cultural context. The results of these exams should inform the leadership selection process for prestigious institutions across America. An emphasis on independent thought will drive our educational processes and focus much like the ACT and SAT have heavily shaped high school curriculums today. Leading people to think for themselves by asking tough questions and demanding thoughtful answers (the Socratic method) is a must. Our current system focuses more on telling what students to think instead of how to think. We need more education on logic, identifying assumptions, formulating a hypothesis, gathering supporting evidence, identifying, and avoiding fallacies, and crafting sound arguments.

- Encourage an individual approach to career counseling beginning in early school education years. Students should receive opportunities to develop their unique skills when they do not fit the mold of traditional educational goals and objectives.

- As previously discussed, we must put an end to generational poverty and dysfunctional neighborhoods. These negative forces snuff the dreams and initiative of millions of children who might otherwise contribute much to American greatness.

CHAPTER 10

Work Harder not Smarter

Until we can manage time, we can manage nothing else.
—Peter Drucker

THERE IS A CRISIS in America—workaholics are fenagling their way into leadership positions across institutions of every type and dragging the work force with them. Creativity, vision, and innovative thought have been replaced by the willingness to sacrifice everything else in life for career success. Climbing to the top in large organizations is now most strongly correlated with the amount of time a person is willing to spend on the job. Nevertheless, quantity of time does not equal quality; routinely burning the midnight oil does not make you a more effective leader. In fact, just the opposite is usually the case. Everyone dreads working for a boss who treats time on the job as an unlimited commodity, but these leaders are also those who most often climb to the top. After all, it is very difficult to outperform someone who places no bounds on the effort they are willing to expend to fulfill their objectives—or so it might appear. In order to assess their effectiveness, it is instructive to first review various types of workaholics as well as their methods and motives. Here are a few whom you will likely to recognize:

The Control Freak: This person must be involved in every decision no matter how small; micro-managers to the nth degree. They do not delegate responsibility to subordinates and retain approval authority for every important decision. He must, therefore, do his job and that of his subordinates as well. Instead of empowering 3 to 6 subordinate leaders, the control freak has 3 to 6 action officers who bring him all manner of information required to manage the entire enterprise. This is an incredibly inefficient way of doing business that requires extended hours—the control freak drags his team kicking and screaming with him into the wee hours of the evening. He probably rose to a position of authority by being a no-holds-bared worker who always accomplished the mission, but never learned how to delegate, empower, train, motivate and trust subordinates to get the job done. The control freak is quickly promoted beyond his capability to manage large organizations and the workday therefore continues to get longer as he climbs through the ranks while struggling to maintain complete control. He greatly inhibits the development of his subordinates by preventing them from thinking or acting independently.

The Coward: Absolutely will not make a decision that involves taking risk unless forced into a corner. Would rather delay, delay, and delay some more until the issue is overcome by events and he therefore cannot be blamed for the outcome of unpredictable events. Loves passive voice as this diffuses responsibility: "Events unfolded too quickly to respond, mistakes were made", etc. Usually manifests as a "detailed oriented" leader—he must know all the facts bearing on a problem before rushing to a decision. His team routinely burns the midnight oil answering a never-ending stream of trivial questions which allows the leader to defer making the required decisions; meetings extend into the late PM. This style frustrates talented subordinates who flee the organization at first opportunity. Junior leaders seek mentors outside of the organization and will attempt to go around the coward to get the decisions they need to accomplish their work in a timely fashion.

The Hero: Must outwork everyone and provide more apparent value to the organization than all others. The most visible metric to superiors is time spent on the job and this type of leader goes out of his way to ensure that everyone knows that he is at work earlier and/or later than anyone else. Routinely sends out emails while most other people are at home as evidence of his dedication. Expects more out of his team so he routinely has them work overtime and ensures that upper management knows about this activity. Rarely if ever gives credit or recognizes subordinates—everything is about him. Lacks emotional intelligence because he is a narcissist and therefore expects his team to mirror his dedication while pledging unconditional loyalty to him.

The Politician: This person believes that everything is about relationships and popularity. He works extremely hard at ensuring that his superiors view him in a positive light. Does not care much about the actual work being done by his team as that is not what will get him promoted—how superiors feel about him is all that matters. Goes out of his way to schmooze those above him; will likely play golf with senior management on the weekends, volunteer his team for every high-visibility activity such as corporate fundraisers and will perform personal favors for his boss. Abuses his team whenever things go off track or put him in a negative light. Routinely holds the team after hours to get updates on work progress because he spends most of the day kissing butts instead of leading, but also recognizes the need to appear to be dedicated.

The Weasel: Views his position as a competition and is not interested in accomplishing anything except kissing up to superiors and throwing his peers under the bus. Everything is about making himself look good and others look bad—damn the moral or ethical implications. Does not necessarily work long-hours but goes to great lengths to appear that he does. Will routinely drop in on senior management late in the evening to catch up with the boss and slyly spread negative rumors and inuendo about his peers. The wrong kind of boss enjoys gaining this inside information and thus over-values the weasel instead of throwing him out of his office. The weasel works hard at catching the boss at opportune times to spread his poison.

The Incompetent: This is a person who finds himself in a position for which he has neither the organizational experience nor the technical competence to properly perform his duties but is nevertheless conscientious and interested in doing the right thing. He therefore demands that his team teach him the fundamentals necessary to make good decisions instead of merely accepting their advice. The incompetent leader manifests as someone who demands "pre-briefs" and extensive preparatory work before making a decision or engaging with higher authority. While this leader has the right stuff in terms of motivation and work-ethic, he has been promoted beyond his capabilities and is simply making the best out of a bad situation. Instead of letting go and allowing the organization to function in spite of his ignorance, he demands to be involved and the workday thus extends well into the PM while he plays catch-up.

Few workaholics fit perfectly into one of the aforementioned descriptions; there are many possible hybrids. The Political weasel, and Incompetent coward traits for instance often combine to create a unique cocktail for whom it is never fun or rewarding to work.

Do any of the above sound like people for whom you would like to work? I doubt it, but many of us are trapped in the tyranny of organizations led by workaholics and cannot easily escape. Not only do they own the present and control the battle-rhythm of the office, they also determine the future by selecting and promoting those cast in their own image. Misery loves company and there is nothing like another workaholic with whom to rationalize the need to work late while everyone else has long since gone home. Those other slackers simply do not understand the burden of senior leadership and they never will......or so the workaholics convince themselves. What is impossible for them to know is how well their teams would perform if they strove to be more efficient and focused upon increasing their decision velocity.

Time is the most precious fixed quantity which a leader spends; an hour spent doing x is an hour not spent doing y. Effective time management is therefore a leadership fundamental, but the workaholic will never see it this way by making tradeoffs. He will simply take as much time as necessary to accomplish both x and y even if it requires working excessively late on a routine basis. If one treats work-imposed time as an unlimited quantity, then there is no need to set and communicate organizational priorities. This results in the all too familiar culture of simply grinding through all the work in the pipeline versus making conscious choices regarding what must be done immediately versus what can be deferred for another day. If everything is equally important, however, there can be no vision for the future as this requires prioritizing efforts and realigning resources needed to affect change to achieve new objectives. Workaholics, therefore, manifest as visionless bureaucrats who drive their organizations to simply maintain the current routine—they are incapable of changing anything of real consequence except perhaps the length of the workday.

Unfortunately, those who get the job done when they are junior leaders rapidly advance through the ranks. Individuals who fight their way to the top are usually the most accomplished doers of deeds. True leadership, however, requires the delegation of authority. What the head of a large organization can accomplish in a single day counts for nothing compared to the acts of his subordinates. Delegation requires giving away authority, control and holding subordinates accountable for their actions. Many would-be leaders struggle with delegating for various reasons, but for workaholics, it is often easier to simply do a task themselves rather than delegate. As a leader develops and progresses, however, the requisite skillset must evolve from actively doing to primarily thinking. A senior leader must constantly contemplate how to optimize organizational performance, modify processes, place the right personnel in crucial positions, and communicate strategic goals and direction. But for the workaholic, taking time to think gets in the way of doing and such a person can therefore never realize their full potential as a leader. It is far more effective to have a lazy intellectual as the CEO of a major corporation than to have a dim-witted workaholic. The intellectual will take time to think about strategic direction even in the face of a crisis while the workaholic will simply busy himself rearranging the chairs on the deck of the Titanic. The crux of the dilemma lies in the fact that intellectuals, lazy or not, take a backseat to the most accomplished doers of deeds early in their careers. Creativity, intelligence, and innovative thought are too often bred out of the ranks in favor of task accomplishment.

One final point regarding workaholics merits consideration. The various types discussed above all suffer from flaws in either their motivation or their ability to lead, but just as importantly, they put their careers above everything else in life to include family, friends, hobbies and external interests. They thus tend to be quite dull human beings who are literally "all in" regarding their chosen profession. This is dangerous and should be viewed as such because these individuals are far more likely to have moral or ethical lapses in judgement compared to individuals who strive for a more balanced lifestyle. When presented with a dilemma that requires doing the harder right over the easier wrong, workaholics carry the emotional burden imposed by the fact that they have put all of life's eggs into the career basket. Such a person will struggle to do the right thing if it conflicts with their career ambitions. The higher up the careerist climbs, the more dangerous these potential lapses in judgement become as they can bring shame and discredit upon the entire organization.

We have examined how workaholics often fail to set clear priorities and organizational goals, inhibit subordinate development, drive away junior talent, crush morale and resilience and are prone to making unethical decisions. Any organization interested in sustainable success, therefore, would do well to implement measures to prevent workaholics from rising to positions of considerable influence. First and foremost, routinely working absurdly long hours needs to be viewed as a badge of shame not of honor—there must be something wrong with the leaders' approach, ability, or motivation if this is necessary. Senior management should require supervisors to justify the need to work overtime. Organizations should close their doors and shut down their email and IT platforms soon after normal operating hours to take away the workaholics' ability to extend the workday indefinitely. Having these tools and access reactivated would require senior leader approval to be granted only in the case of true emergencies. Finally, advancement through the ranks must account for both general and job specific intelligence. Many organizations are loathe to implement such measures as some senior leaders would inevitably be found wanting in this domain. Nevertheless, leading is primarily a thinking persons' game and you can neither incentivize that which you do not measure nor can you lead in a domain that you do not understand. The control freaks, cowards, heroes, weasels, politicians, and incompetents must be culled from the herd. Workaholics reading this will gnash their teeth in scorn and provide long lists of accomplishments achieved through dedication and commitment as evidence that they have the best approach to leading. The unknowable variable, however, is how much an organization might have accomplished if more intelligent, and creative individuals who spend more time thinking than doing were in charge. The time is ripe to bring balance back to the work force and unleash its full innovative potential—workaholics need not apply!

Proposed Reforms

- View excessive time on the job as ineffective leadership. It should be a badge of shame not honor.

- Carefully monitor leaders who routinely burn the midnight oil and implement measures to prevent them from dragging the workforce down with them. Controlling after hours access to office spaces and IT networks limits the workaholics' ability to create a perpetual workday.

CHAPTER 11

Leadership Specialties

The main insight learned from interdisciplinary studies is the return to specialization.
—George Stigler

A S PREVIOUSLY DISCUSSED, EVERYONE does not possess the qualities to effectively lead. Even for those who do have the appropriate attributes, they are best suited for specific leadership roles. Every seasoned soldier, for instance, recognizes the difference between a good leader in the garrison environment versus an effective leader in the field or combat setting. The contrast in performance results from varying personal attributes, interests, and experiences. The Army needs highly capable leaders in both these domains. The field and garrison, however, represent only a fraction of the entire service. The institutional Army, for instance, exists to train, equip, sustain, and support combat formations but has very little in common with tactical units. Oddly, individuals who excel at leading battalions, brigades, and divisions are also entrusted to lead the institutional Army. In order to understand the shortcomings of this approach, consider the analogy below.

Imagine a professional football team comprised entirely of players who were great all-around athletes. Every position would be occupied by a person who would weigh approximately 220 pounds, run quickly, and have above average physical strength. Nobody, however, would have particularly unique talents or attributes; a team of decathletes if you will. Let this club meet an opponent of specialists with wide receivers who were blazing fast, a quarterback who could throw bombs, 300-pound lineman whom the generalists would simply bounce off, and a relatively frail person who could kick 55-yard field goals. How do you think that game would go? The team of decathletes would most assuredly be the laughingstock of the league. Special roles require special talents; there is no one-size fits all athlete for any sport.

Leadership resembles football in this respect. Individuals who seek to lead have varying personal skills, interests, and experiences, and are therefore suited to serve in different roles to achieve unique results. A great organization focused on achieving optimal performance therefore should educate, train, and utilize leadership specialists because nobody can be great at everything. Any organization treating leaders as interchangeable cogs in the machine capable of filling any role will be outgunned by a competitor team of specialists. Unfortunately, leadership is viewed almost exclusively as a general set of skills, and not just by the Army. If you do not believe it, conduct an internet search on the term "leadership specialties", and as of the writing of this in July 2020, you will get exactly zero relevant hits. The discussion below is an attempt to change the collective thinking on this matter and introduce leadership specialties into the vernacular as well as highlight the implications for large organizations.

Before tackling special roles, however, we must consider the fundamental building blocks of leadership. At its core, leadership is the art of influencing others to achieve desired outcomes. Every organization has both leaders and followers and one of the key discriminators between the two is ambition. A leader must possess the drive to invest more energy to achieving results than followers as he is entrusted with more power and is also usually more richly rewarded than members of the team. For a group to accept the guidance of a leader, this person must have institutional credibility as well as exceptional dedication. Credibility is gained by a thorough understanding of the environment in which the leader operates. Technical and organizational mastery as well as commitment, therefore, form the foundational basis required to exert influence.

One cannot lead that which he does not understand! Most organizations overlook this fundamental and view leadership as a generic set of skills to be applied in any domain. If one extends this logic to the extreme, however, it results in the conclusion that Mark Zuckerberg (founder of Facebook) and Bill Belichick (head football coach for the New England Patriots) could easily switch roles without perturbing their respective organizations given both are highly accomplished leaders. We intuitively know this simply does not hold true because the two are experts who lead within domains foreign to each other and possess radically varied skills and experiences. Additionally, they must focus on achieving different results given the nature of their respective businesses. The idea that leadership is leadership regardless of the domain is intellectually shallow, but convenient for organizations not willing to invest in tailored utilization and development.

Leaders come in endless permutations, but the four roles listed below are common regardless of the technical domain. All four roles: 1) Team Builder, 2) Sustainer, 3) Crisis Manager, and 4) Innovator are essential to ensure enduring success for any large organization and merit detailed consideration.

Team Builder: This person focuses on individual employee development and collective training. The role requires leaders with significant human intelligence and intrapersonal skills, as well as the broad organizational knowledge and experiences required to assess and align individual skillsets with the appropriate positions. The team builder is an expert trainer who drives a close-knit organization with high morale focused on accomplishing objectives.

Cornerstone Personal Interest:

Skill improvement and training; pursuit of personal excellence.

Sustainer: Focus on keeping the organization operating at a high output level by optimizing processes. This role requires leaders with organizational genius, attention to detail, and a high level of personal energy to drive the task organization and team supervision necessary to achieve success. The team builder crafts the building blocks for the organization while the sustainer creates and manages the structure to deliver impressive results.

Cornerstone Personal Interest:

Efficiency; student of organizational processes.

Crisis Manager: Focus on properly handling unforeseen emergencies to prevent organizational disasters. This role requires leaders capable of making rapid decisions with the self-confidence required to accept and manage high risk activities. Results in a flexible and confident organization postured to adapt to changing situations. The crisis manager has a calming effect on the organization and successfully navigates hardships.

Cornerstone Personal Interest:

Bringing order out of chaos; comfortable with high risk activities.

Innovator: Focus on the future and anticipates evolving conditions requiring adaptation. This role demands intensively inquisitive leaders with high levels of creativity and imagination. Results in an organization capable of generating new and useful ideas and is comfortable with change. The innovator generates the ideas necessary for success tomorrow while most other leaders are focused upon the business at hand today.

Cornerstone Personal Interest:

> **Cutting-edge applications; creative genius, dreamer.**

Figure 4 on the following page provides a graphical depiction of the relationships and importance of organizational and technical experiences, personal interests, leadership specialty roles as well as their associated results—the leadership "house" upon which enduring success is built. The ideal core leadership team of any large organization would consist of specialists of every variety who were deliberately prepared to serve in their respective roles. The Chief Executive Officer (CEO) might be a Team Builder, the Chief Financial Officer (CFO) a Sustainer, the Chief Technology Officer (CTO) an Innovator, and the Chief Operating Officer (COO) a Crisis Manager, but the role played by each position is far less important than having coverage of all areas.

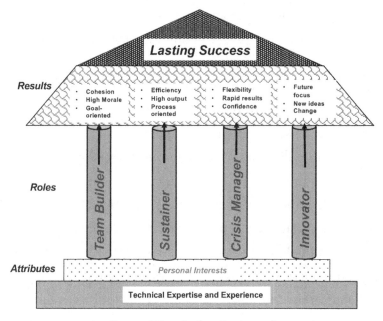

Figure 4: Leadership Framework

Development, Assignment and Retention of Specialists:

Identifying who has the talents and personal interests to serve in the various leadership specialties poses a challenge because many attributes are intangible, qualitative properties which are difficult to measure or assess. The most straightforward and effective approach, therefore, is to simply ask would-be leaders to self-identify which role would best optimize their talents and interests at the outset of their careers. People usually know themselves far better than their supervisors or human resources departments, but individuals also change with age and experience so the appropriate roles must be periodically reevaluated. Recalling that blooming leaders usually possess significant ambition, an organization must carefully consider its incentive structure and institutional values. If it values creativity above all other attributes, for instance, then the leaders who climb to the top of the pyramid will almost exclusively be Innovators thus producing a senior management cohort that possesses very similar experiences and competencies while lacking diversity of thought and leadership approach. Such a group might patent remarkable new inventions yet lack the competencies to effectively manage an exploding enterprise and market its products. The lack of leaders capable of serving in all four roles results in groupthink, blind-spots and imbalances which prevent enduring organizational success as demonstrated in Figure 4. None of the four roles above is less important than another nor can any of these leadership specialties be outsourced to external agencies.

The four major leadership roles attract and require individuals with varying attributes and interests. Both Innovators and Team builders, for instance, tend to lead with an eye towards setting the conditions for future success by focusing their efforts on planning and preparation while Crisis Managers and Sustainers operate very much in the here and now and execute immediate priorities. Another important distinction lies in the relative importance of individual contributions versus collective efforts. Innovators and Crisis Managers rely more upon individual talents while Team Builders and Sustainers have a group-centric orientation. Figure 5 on the following page depicts these relationships in a quadrant format.

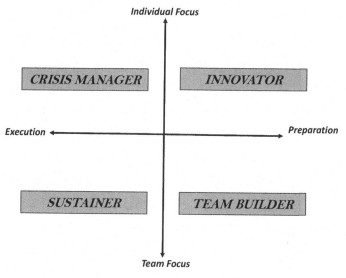

Figure 5: Leader Orientation

Understanding the likely fundamental orientation of various leadership specialties is important because of its relationship to talents, personal interests, roles, and organizational values. If an organization puts a premium on selfless service above all other attributes, for instance, it may unwittingly cull Innovators and Crisis Managers from the leadership herd given their tendencies to rely more heavily upon their individual skills and genius. Alternatively, if an organization continually chases the next good idea to be first to market, this exclusively future-looking posture will probably drive away Crisis Managers, and Sustainers more focused on delivering immediate results. Every organization, therefore, must carefully balance its values and incentive structures to allow room on the bus for leaders capable in all roles.

Case Study

The United States Army provides an excellent example of an organization with values and a leadership development process which do not produce leadership specialists. General Officers sit atop the professional pyramid—emphasis on the word general. Upon graduating from college or a military academy, most newly commissioned officers interested in a life-long military career chose a path to maximize their promotion potential to one day reach the exalted General Officer ranks. After all, most new Lieutenants are ferociously ambitious, or they would not have chosen and successfully navigated challenging commissioning programs. The assignment sequence to reach the top (four-star level) requires officers to continually hone their team building skills with an occasional dash of crisis management also known as combat operations. The sheer grind of the Army career path characterized by numerous geographical reassignments, fourteen-hour days while in Garrison, and frequent family separation emphasizes selfless service above all other attributes. In short, the Army officer developmental process and incentive structure serves as a sieve under-valuing and filtering out individuals with the attributes and interests to serve as Innovators and Sustainers—essential roles in managing the institutional Army with little direct relationship to preparing and leading maneuver units for combat. An Army officer who does not spend most of his career in combat units will likely never have the opportunity to lead at the corporate four-star level of the Service. The

Army does not acknowledge the need for leadership specialties at this level and does not create unique career paths to maximize an individual's personal interests and attributes; it is a one-size fits all paradigm very similar to the football team of decathletes. How many Army equivalents of Tom Brady have wasted their lives trying to play on the defensive line instead of self-actualizing as quarterbacks because leadership is viewed in such a generic sense?

Army officers are graded in every assignment and lukewarm performance in a single position will end one's career ascent. Unfortunately, a would-be Innovator, for instance, must compete against Team Builders and Crisis Managers early in his career while gaining a baseline experience in operational units. The evaluation criteria in these early roles heavily favor combat leaders and thus result in a handicap for anyone who does not fit the mold and possess the competencies, interests, and desire to serve in this capacity. Such experiences disenfranchise and frustrate officers with other talents and interests neither recognized nor needed in these formative assignments. This provides strong incentive to depart service early and seek civilian employment.

Unfortunately, the Army currently desperately needs Innovators as 18 years of the Global War on Terror have dulled our sword. The tanks, helicopters, missiles, armored vehicles, and individual weapons our soldiers employ today are largely built upon the same basic technologies that existed when the first variants were fielded in the 1980s. The United

States Army no longer has a technological advantage over our most dangerous and capable adversaries. Additionally, the war fighting doctrine, tactics and techniques required to face anything but low-level asymmetrical threats such as terrorism have not been updated in a generation. In response to these shortcomings, the Army created a four-star Futures Command chartered to lead the development of the next generation of dominant weapon systems and then recruited a senior leadership team from a group of General Officers most of whom never had a single assignment remotely correlate with Innovation. Most of these Generals also do not have the appropriate technical backgrounds, personal attributes, or interests to serve in those roles. Recall that they "signed up" to be team builders and crisis managers—combat formation leaders. Performing well in this domain catapulted them to high command, but the Army now finds itself with a scarcity of the senior leadership talent it needs to drive the appropriate changes in weapons and war fighting doctrine.

Recruiting, developing and retaining capable specialty leaders willing and able to perform as Innovators is still not an Army priority, and they unfortunately cannot be molded from the wrong type of clay—individuals who lack the interest, personal attributes and experiences necessary to perform this crucial function. This will not end well for the Army or the nation; billions of dollars and precious time will be wasted before Congress has the data it needs to put an end to this nonsense—the root cause of which is an intellectually lazy view of leadership as a general set of skills. A Crisis Manager forced to serve as an Innovator, for instance, will likely look for "quick wins" to tough technical challenges in an attempt to rapidly solve problems—he is a hammer who views every problem as a nail to immediately drive. Predictably, this only leads to wasting precious time and resources on throw-away solutions as innovation requires foresight, patience, long-term commitment, and investment.

Sensing this crisis and the need for change, the Defense Innovation Board (DIB) composed of a wide variety of academic and industry experts recently recommended that the Department of Defense (DOD) implement a STEM (Science, Technology, Engineering, and Mathematics) career field to recruit and retain these specialty competencies.[36] While this may sound insightful, there is no discussion regarding how these STEM experts would be used and who in uniform would lead them. What the DIB experts such as Neil DeGrasse Tyson (renowned astrophysicist) lack is institutional perspective. They cannot fully understand the fact that the DOD has an anti-intellectual cultural bias because they never served a day in uniform and therefore possess limited context. Nevertheless, these industry and academic experts correctly identify that every organization must possess homegrown Innovators and the DOD desperately needs to create the conditions conducive

---

36 Aaron Mehta, *Pentagon tech advisors want special career track, "innovation elevator" for big thinkers*, Military Times, October 26, 2017.

to producing and retaining these specialty leaders. Innovators need to be immersed in DOD culture and thoroughly familiar with every aspect of the institution but provided a separate career path not requiring them to compete with knuckle-dragging, door-kicking war fighters—Team Builders and Crisis Managers. These individuals are the team's offensive line if you will, but they should exist to provide the Quarterback, an Innovator, the time, and space needed to "go deep".

The DOD currently possesses a sprawling network of labs and research, development, and engineering centers with tens of thousands of STEM experts, but what it lacks are senior uniformed leaders capable of leading them and leveraging their contributions. Back to the fundamental: you cannot lead that which you do not understand. Change must be driven from the top—particularly for an organization like DOD placing a premium on compliance with disincentives to disagree because this flirts with the most repugnant of institutional violations (disobedience). DOD might begin to address the desperately needed and long overdue changes by acknowledging the existence and potential payoff of leadership specialties. Leaders who can drive innovation possess starkly different individual competencies and personal interests than those who chose to serve in combat roles. Innovators must be groomed with a series of institutional assignments and experiences which incrementally prepare them to lead at the enterprise level of the Service. While leading people who do the Nation's bidding at the tip of the spear so to speak is incredibly important, it is absurd to believe this prepares one to make good decisions about the complex technologies resident in next-generation weapon systems or to lead the very technical teams who build them. The Army would never place a PhD scientist who spent his entire career working in a Defense Laboratory in command of an Infantry Brigade in combat, but the converse is guaranteed under its current incentive and promotion structure.

Nevertheless, the Army's Future Command could eventually evolve into a more focused and useful engine for change. As the consequences of assigning combat leaders to oversee the development of the next generation of weapon systems slowly manifest themselves, this will encourage the Army to create a cohort of senior leaders selected for their technical competence and provided the experiences necessary to succeed as Innovators. The United States will win or lose the next major war with a peer competitor based upon intelligence, surveillance, and reconnaissance capabilities as well as weapons that operate in space and the cyber domain. While Airborne Rangers and Special Operations Forces may be the most effective options in today's Army toolbox, they will likely be largely irrelevant in the next major conflict— "geeks" will likely lead our future National Defense. Given the fact it takes thirty years or more to grow a four-star General, the Army had best begin to recruit and retain a cohort of leadership specialists capable of driving innovation as a matter of utmost importance.

In an age of ever-increasing specialization, does it not seem odd that leadership continues to be viewed as a general set of skills? Nearly every career field has exploded into ever more refined and detailed occupations. Take the practice of medicine for instance—there are hundreds of specialized career fields today where only a few generations ago there were merely general practitioners, researchers, and surgeons. I certainly would not seek the help of a dermatologist to treat a degenerative spinal column in the same manner I would not expect a lifelong crisis manager to drive technological innovations. The time is ripe to implement leadership specialties given the potential benefits. Not only will private businesses and government agencies become more efficient and competitive, but individual leaders will maximize their chances of reaching their full potential. Before committing to a career, the acknowledgement of leadership specialties will encourage individuals to first consider their unique talents and interests, what roles best leverage these, and whether the endeavor they are joining will value and fully reward their long-term contributions. There are a very few exceptionally talented individuals who can perform well in almost any role, but most of us have a subset of the full universe of leadership talents and attributes. Where do you fit in and what leadership roles suit you best?

Proposed Reforms

- Implement the concept of leadership specialties in large organizations and provide separate career tracks for team builders, innovators, crisis managers and sustainers.

• The DOD should stand up a think tank consisting of highly intelligent officers who have the skills and attributes to serve as Innovators. These officers should periodically rotate between conventional line assignments and the think tank throughout the depth of their careers and have a path to service at the four-star corporate level of all Services. These officers should study and collaborate on important issues such as the military implications of technological innovations, emerging threats, and future warfighting doctrine.

CHAPTER 12

Thank you for your Service

I believe that we are here for each other, not against each other. Everything comes from an understanding that you are a gift in my life—whoever you are, whatever our differences.

—John Denver

"THANK YOU FOR YOUR service" has become perhaps one of the most common phrases in American culture. Many use it to show gratitude and in so doing, believe this somehow exempts them from any responsibility to serve their country. Perhaps this is why the above phrase has always made me a little uncomfortable despite having retired after nearly thirty years in the military. It is not that I do not appreciate the sentiment. I just never really felt like I deserved special recognition; particularly since I was never wounded in combat.

Everyone's story is different—mine began when I enlisted in the Army as a young person with little else going for me. I subsequently benefited mightily from all the wonderful opportunities associated with uniformed service. The United States Army trained, educated, and promoted me while providing generous compensation and professional recognition. Along the way, I had the chance to do things that I loved while forming enriching personal and professional relationships. I lacked for nothing. When first greeted with this perhaps over-used phrase (thank you for your service), I turned red with embarrassment. Surely you can't be talking to me. I have since thought deeply about what people are really trying to convey when they use this phrase, and what follows is an attempt to widen the perspective on the matter.

Most Americans have a sense of respect for individuals who sacrifice. Now that is an important word—sacrifice. It is almost synonymous with service in our everyday lexicon. My wife Rachel could teach us much about this concept as can the spouses of most career military people. When we married some 25 years ago, she was young, beautiful (still is), talented, and full of energy; simply unlimited potential! Neither of us understood what we were getting into as I endeavored to be a "lifer" in the Army. Our first assignment together was with the 82nd Airborne Division far away from all family and friends; quite an eye-opening experience. I was deployed on military training exercises roughly half of the time, and the other half consisted of grueling 14-hour work days that left me physically spent and almost always late for dinner. We had a Battalion Commander who put a cot in his office and refused to go home to his wife and children during the work week. In his opinion, our national security hung in the balance in 1995—how ridiculous that seems now looking back! How could we possibly be ready for war if we did not dedicate our every waking moment to the "mission"? He would walk around our barracks and offices at 7 pm to see who was still at work. Those Officers who were not present at this late hour, he punished with negative evaluation reports. "If the Army wanted you to have a spouse, it would have issued you one" was the prevailing sentiment. If an individual does not care enough about his children to make time for them, why should we trust him to lead America's sons and daughters in combat?

Despite this negative encounter, I was living the dream—learning, training, and practicing the art of military leadership; my cup was full. My wife, however, experienced a very lonely existence far-removed from family support and friendship while wed to a mostly absent husband. We were young and in love, however, so we made it work by treasuring holiday leave and long weekends. As the years piled up, we were blessed with three wonderful children. She tended to their every need, turned her back on her own significant career opportunities, and existed solely to support me, our children, and the less fortunate military families of whatever unit in which we happened to serve at the moment. Compared to her, I know nothing of sacrifice! When a well-meaning fellow citizen recognizes me and thanks me for my service in the presence of my wife, therefore, I quite naturally feel ashamed. Please bypass me and thank her; she is far more deserving of your appreciation!

Sacrifice is not the only element of service. Many Americans also use the phrase to acknowledge that military members voluntarily risk their lives as the threat of armed conflict is an ever-present reality. When I enlisted in the 1980s, the Cold War raged and there seemed little chance of engaging in combat. I certainly did not sign up "to fight and die" for my country even though I recognized this as a distant possibility. Yes, being a Soldier, Sailor, Airman or Marine incurs a level of risk to life and limb that most Americans do not share, but how is that any different than what our first responders (Police, Firefighters, Coast Guard, Medical trauma units, Homeland Security and Disaster assistance teams) do for all American citizens? It's not really—the distinction is artificial. They and their families sacrifice and take risks on behalf of all of us. Every American directly benefits from their dedication and professionalism and can count on their help in an instant by simply dialing 911. If you want to thank me for my service and I happen to be in the vicinity of one of these professionals, I will again feel embarrassed and ashamed; they are at least as deserving of your praise and gratitude.

The military defends our nation and many Americans use "thank you for your service" to express gratitude for those who willingly accept this responsibility. What most do not consider, however, is that the United States Department of Defense (DoD) consists of a very diverse team that includes not only uniformed personnel, but also federal employees and contractors. Government civilians and contractors perform a considerable portion of the DoD's institutional support functions to include acquiring and managing the development of weapons systems, training and sustaining the force, medical services, and human resources to name but a few. Many of these individuals also routinely deploy into harm's way to more directly support combat operations when needed. As part of the DoD team, these individuals contribute much to the defense of our nation and are also deserving of recognition.

What about the professionals who work within the defense industrial base to design all manner of equipment for the DoD? There are tens of thousands of organizational and innovative geniuses who work around the clock to deliver better body armor, communications systems, individual weapons, ground combat vehicles, aircraft, ships, satellites and missiles to ensure that our young men and women can dominate our enemies. Even as you read this , there are Americans preparing to kick in doors and stare directly into the face of evil. Whether or not they succeed and return home safely depends largely upon the battlefield intelligence, weapons, and protective gear produced by our defense industrial base. The individuals who dedicate their lives and considerable talents to these endeavors are of course a crucial component to the successful defense of our nation—thank them for their service as well.

The categories of Americans discussed above are by no means the complete list of those who deserve thanks. Americans also use the phrase "thank you for your service" to express patriotism. They view military members as the embodiment of our national identity and "thank you for your service" has become the civilian version of "Hooah" if you will—used often to simply express enthusiasm. Patriotism, pride in your national identity, resembles the affection that members of sports teams feel for each other. Camaraderie grows through shared experiences, hardships, and pride in group accomplishments. Every citizen in the United States is a member of Team America; patriotism is simply team spirit. Highly successful teams treat every member with dignity, respect and acknowledge that even the proverbial "towel boy" plays an important role. So why should Team America be any different? Despite the protective bubbles that some privileged Americans construct around themselves, what each of us does impacts all others as well as the overall success of our nation—our fates are inextricably intertwined. If you are a true patriot, there should be no such thing as an unwanted or irrelevant citizen. The Team Captains, the most wealthy and powerful Americans, share the heaviest burden to make our country a success and must actively mentor junior players while seeking to elevate their game.

Taking a wider view of patriotism as national team spirit and acknowledging the contributions of all citizens has the power to positively transform our society. The single parent who loves her children with every fiber of her being while steering them away from violence and crime in a sea of deviant behavior is a patriot. The teacher who dedicates his life to educating our children and making them better citizens is a patriot. The professional athlete who risks fortune and fame to take a stance against social injustice is a patriot. The teenager who stocks groceries after school to help her family make ends meet while striving to save for college is a patriot. The person who removes your garbage with a smile while high fiving all the kids in the neighborhood is a patriot. No matter who you are or what you do, you are a valued and important member of Team America.

Now is an excellent time to not only thank our service members, but also reflect upon the benefits of living in the United States—after all, isn't this what we are fighting for? The state of our Union needs attention perhaps more urgently than the 140 nations across the globe in which we now have "boots on the ground". Unless we are willing to forfeit the future, we must continue to strive for domestic peace, tranquility, justice for all, and provide a safe education system that works for every child no matter the circumstances of their birth. I remain incredibly grateful that I was born in the United States where people are free, willing to sacrifice and take risks on behalf of others, can prosper, and are proud of their country. Ensuring that all our children and subsequent generations can say the same requires a national team effort that leverages the talents and energy of all citizens—not just military servicemembers.

If we do not come together to improve everyone's quality of life within our borders, then we will soon have a country that is not worth defending. We are all in this together. Thanks in advance for your service!

Proposed Reform

- Unconditionally love and respect each other. Strive to accomplish random acts of kindness as often as possible. Insist on leaders who bring us together.

Conclusion

THANK YOU SO MUCH for taking the time to read and really think about these important issues. I have spent countless nights staring at unfamiliar stars pondering conventional wisdom just to pass the time. The life of a career soldier with long periods of solitude and loneliness has taught me much. I wrestled with sharing some of these thoughts because they put institutions I dearly love in a negative light—both our country and its Army. These are only broken at the top, however, and we can easily fix this. Perhaps the strongest theme underlying our *Patriotic Illusions* is incompetent and corrupt leadership. It is long past time to hold our leaders accountable for their actions.

I hope I have offered an alternative view of patriotism which resonates with your experiences and sensibilities. At its core, I believe patriotism is about love for each other: our families, our neighbors, our communities, and our country at large. It is not about fireworks, parades, wars, and unconditional support for the military. We must not allow those with ulterior motives to leverage our deep affections for their self-serving purposes. We all want to live in peace and harmony but hero-worshiping our military leaders who promote neverending wars does not guarantee our safety. In fact, quite the opposite is the case. War destabilizes the international order.

We must also reexamine the politicians who we have placed in power with fresh eyes. They have failed us and will continue to do so until we demand better. Sociopaths and narcists who forfeit everything in life to succeed are not patriots. They lack the prerequisite love for others. We need to seek people across the entire spectrum of our society with inquisitive minds who can solve problems and are willing to take the risks associated with championing change. Our political system must be modified to allow room on the bus for everyone, not just the privileged few born into generational wealth and power. As discussed in great detail, true leaders possess unique attributes. They are very special human beings who are often neither rich nor famous and enter this world under both the best and the worst circumstances imaginable.

In order to create a leadership pipeline to better serve our country, we can begin by teaching our children HOW to think not WHAT to think. The first step is promoting an atmosphere of tolerance in our schools while encouraging individuality, creativity and yes, even respectful disobedience. We must also restore the light of the American dream to every street in the United States whether it be our inner cities wracked with crime and violence or our remote, sparsely populated rural communities crippled by abject poverty.

All these things we can do if only we agree to work together for the common good, not just what is best for ourselves in the here and now. Count yourselves lucky to have been born in the United States. I certainly do. I am proud to be an American and will work the rest of my days on Earth to ensure my children, your children, our children inherit a country better than the one handed down to us.

I realize that many people will take issue with my various proposed reforms. Everyone has a different perspective based on their unique attributes and experiences. I do not claim to have all the answers, not by a longshot! I hope the ideas I offer, however, will ignite a national level dialogue regarding desperately needed change. We need to hear from you. Please connect with me on social media to join the discussion.

Very Respectfully,
Mark Talbot

About the Author

MARK TALBOT IS a writer, entrepreneur, and former career soldier dedicated to a lifetime of service to the United States. He is the President and Founder of T5 Solutions LLC—a Veteran Owned Small Business supporting the development of the next generation of weapons systems. Mark retired as a Colonel after nearly 30 years of diverse enlisted and commissioned service in the Army. His assignments include border patrol in West Germany, numerous leadership positions in the airborne infantry, a Ranger school instructor, an associate engineering professor at West Point, combat service in Iraq, counter-terrorism work within the Intelligence Community, General's aid at the Pentagon, assistant to the US Ambassador to the United Kingdom, and program management of multi-billion dollar advanced defense research efforts. Mark is an honor graduate from West Point, a master parachutist, and holds a master's degree in environmental engineering from the University of North Carolina at Chapel Hill. He is interested in providing new and fresh perspectives regarding leadership, current affairs, and public service. Mark and his wife Rachel have three children and reside in Huntsville, Alabama where they continue to support the Army. Mark and Rachel founded "Climb" in 2019, a 501c3 non-profit organization dedicated to reaching people in need of a helping hand.

Made in the USA
Coppell, TX
06 September 2020